Cybersecurity

This book examines the legal and policy aspects of cybersecurity. It takes a much needed look at cybersecurity from a geopolitical perspective. Through this lens, it seeks to broaden the reader's understanding of the legal and political considerations of individuals, corporations, law enforcement, and regulatory bodies and management of the complex relationships between them. In drawing on interviews conducted with experts from a wide range of fields, the book presents the reader with dilemmas and paradigms that confront lawmakers, corporate leaders, and law enforcement and national leaders. The book is structured in a novel format by employing a series of vignettes, which have been created as exercises intended to confront the reader with the dilemmas involved in cybersecurity. Through the use of vignettes, the work seeks to highlight the constant threat of cybersecurity against various audiences, with the overall aim of facilitating discussion and reaction to actual probable events. In this sense, the book seeks to provide recommendations for best practices in response to the complex and numerous threats related to cybersecurity.

This book will be of interest to students of cybersecurity, terrorism, international law, security studies, and IR in general, as well as policy makers, professionals, and law enforcement officials.

Amos N. Guiora is Professor of Law at the S.J. Quinney College of Law, University of Utah, USA.

'This book provides a fresh and novel perspective on the complex phenomenon that we term "cyberspace." Because of the rise of the world-wide-web as the human communication medium of choice, the internet is no longer a personal, or national space. It embraces us all in a single social bond that has to be both explicated and understood. This is not a "nice to know" situation. It is one that will inevitably require every single individual on this planet to understand how they fit in. This book starts that important conversation and in many ways it is the entry point to reaching that new understanding of borderless, in many cases anonymous and even cultureless human interaction. Careful attention ought to be paid to the concerns raised here. And ideas for dealing with them developed.' — *Daniel Shoemaker, Center for Cyber Security and Intelligence Studies, University of Detroit, Mercy, USA*

'The application of formidable experience and expertise to the scary world of cybersecurity is the hallmark of this book. Amos N. Guiora provides a lively and original approach to delineating this new frontier. He offers illuminating explanations of the threats and devises multi-tiered responses, all firmly grounded in real life situations. His combination of analysis and pragmatism make study of this book a highly rewarding experience.' — *Clive Walker, Professor Emeritus, University of Leeds, UK*

'*Cybersecurity* is both timely and insightful. Amos N. Guiora has done an outstanding job in creating a must-read volume for professionals, law enforcement, policy makers and anyone concerned with the challenges cyber terrorism and cyber crime pose to our increasingly data-driven, interconnected and interdependent society.' — *Michael F. Shapiro, Executive Director, National Cyber Partnership, USA*

Cybersecurity
Geopolitics, law, and policy

Amos N. Guiora

Routledge
Taylor & Francis Group

LONDON AND NEW YORK

First published 2017
by Routledge
2 Park Square, Milton Park, Abingdon, Oxon OX14 4RN

and by Routledge
711 Third Avenue, New York, NY 10017

Routledge is an imprint of the Taylor & Francis Group, an informa business

British Library Cataloguing in Publication Data
A catalogue record for this book is available from the British Library

Library of Congress Cataloging-in-Publication Data
Names: Guiora, Amos N., 1957- author.
Title: Cybersecurity : geopolitics, law, and policy / Amos N. Guiora.
Other titles: Cybersecurity
Description: Boca Raton, FL : Routledge, 2017. | Includes bibliographical references and index.
Identifiers: LCCN 2016041237| ISBN 9781498729116 (hardback) | ISBN 9781138033290 (pbk.) | ISBN 9781315370231 (ebook)
Subjects: LCSH: Computer networks--Security measures--Government policy. | Computer security--Government policy. | Computer crimes--Prevention. | Technology and international relations.
Classification: LCC TK5105.59 .G85 2017 | DDC 005.8--dc23
LC record available at https://lccn.loc.gov/2016041237

ISBN: 978-1-498-72911-6 (hbk)
ISBN: 978-1-138-03329-0 (pbk)
ISBN: 978-1-315-37023-1 (ebk)

Typeset in Sabon
by Taylor & Francis Books

Contents

1 An introduction to cybersecurity

Scary. Confusing. Unsettling.
Threatening. Unseen. Potent.
Disruptive. Invasive.

The list above is but a sample of words associated with **cybersecurity** and **cyberterrorism**. It reflects the lack of uniformity regarding the essence of the terms, specifically less narrow and implementable definitions. Certainly the list above is neither complete nor agreed upon by all. That is obvious. That is the reality of cybersecurity and cyberterrorism.

Clearly cyberterrorism poses significant threats; far from clear is how to respond, whether proactively or reactively. Communication with experts—interspersed throughout this book—highlights this twin reality. Although the threats are broadly understood, there is a lack of unanimity regarding threat minimization.

Conversations with academics, cyber experts, government officials, and corporate leaders in the United States, United Kingdom, and Israel compellingly highlighted this complexity. In exploring this twin reality—threat known; response unclear—I focused on the legal and policy aspects of cybersecurity. I do so because it is impossible to understand cybersecurity exclusively through the lens of one of the two.

The integrated approach—law and policy—is essential to facilitating discussion regarding possible means to counter the threat posed by nefarious use of cyber. What I do not address are the technical-techological aspects of cyber; by design, that is left to others who are more competent to do so. Throughout the writing process, what struck me was a recognition of the threat posed but a sense of answers wanted. Many of my interactions with **cyber professionals**—those engaged in never-ending efforts to counterminimize cyber threats to their customers and clients—focused on tactical measures rather than broad-based, strategic thinking. This is not a criticism, but rather an observation. Perhaps this is a reality of the cyber threat. The emphasis on tactical responses suggests stopgap measures, a *win one day, lose the next day* approach. In many ways, that is akin to traditional operational counterterrorism.

My experience—based on 20 years of service in the Israel Defense Forces, Judge Advocate General's Corps—reflects the reality that operational counterterrorism is more tactical in orientation rather than strategic. It is for this reason that President Obama's promise to *defeat and denigrate ISIS* rang hollow with me. In this vein, there is, then, a symmetry between traditional operational counterterrorism and nascent counter cybersecurity.

Although my professional background is largely in the former, it is highly applicable and relevant to the latter. Some of the legal and policy aspects of counterterrorism are *transferable* to cybersecurity, defining and applying self-defense standards and limits, defining effectiveness of countermeasures, developing and implementing cooperation mechanisms among the affected institutions, educating the public regarding the limits of state power, recognizing the confluence between states and **nonstate actors** (**NSA**), and developing both defensive and offensive instruments to minimize the threats posed.

The importance of definitions cannot be sufficiently emphasized, particularly regarding the establishment of limits of state power (for the reader's convenience, **bolded** terms are further defined in the "Glossary of Terms"). Nation-state actions—preemptive or reactive—are subject to conventions, treaties, and laws. What complicates counter cybersecurity, as compared to traditional operational counterterrorism, is that the intended target may well be a private actor-enterprise, resulting in a critical dilemma: Is the nation-state obligated to act on behalf, for example, of a corporate entity based in its territory? Simply put: Is a cyber attack on an American corporation an attack on America? Distinct from a terrorist attack resulting in physical harm—to persons and property—a cyber attack exacts a cost to infrastructure, financial markets, and personal privacy.

Although physical harm may result, cyber attack is a by-product unlike a physical attack whose intended purpose is to kill innocent individuals. This is, obviously, a significant difference between the two. However, in both, nonstate actors—sometimes with active support and cooperation of nation-states—are consciously seeking to cause harm, whether physical or otherwise. Perhaps, traditional terrorism is easier to process for the harm that is physical and visceral. This is distinct from a well-executed cyber attack whose consequences may not be immediately recognized and understood.

Discussion regarding cybersecurity is marked by discomfort and a sense of foreboding. The many conversations I have had with a wide range of experts in the United States, Israel, and the United Kingdom reflect a sense of *new frontier*. However, unlike positive imagery traditionally associated with new frontiers, the reality is a mixed bag reflecting, more than anything else, concern regarding dangers posed by cybersecurity. That is, the obvious benefits of cyber are mitigated—perhaps offset is a better term—by cyberterrorism.

Hundreds of millions enjoy Facebook, Instagram, text messaging, and other forms of contemporary communication. Similarly, cyber greatly increases our access to information and significantly eases many aspects of our daily lives. This is well-documented and readily apparent. However, it is the *flip* side of cyber that is our focus in this book. Although the benefits are obvious, the question is how to respond to the harm caused by those who use cyber for illegal, harmful, and destructive purposes.

The conversations suggest a sense of foreboding, reflecting uncertainty regarding the specific nature of future attacks but certainty regarding their inevitability. This duality was highlighted for me in a conversation I had in May 2016 with a senior executive of an American corporation that had recently been hacked. The executive shared with me that the hack was truly speaking no surprise and reflected the consequences of a calculated decision. The corporation had been aware that hacking was a distinct possibility but that prevention was expensive and burdensome.

Therefore, the C level decided to *roll the dice* and invest in minimal protection and hope that a hack, were it to occur, would not be, in his words, *overwhelming*. This means that the corporation was willing to tolerate a hack but not willing to invest significant financial assets to protect itself. Simply put: some protection with limited resources was allocated as compared to significant protection with maximum responses. It was, admittedly, a gamble.

The consequences are significant at multiple levels: financial, customer concern, and public image. However, I was particularly struck by his assessment of the three costs, particularly regarding customer reaction. The executive shared with me that customers were less concerned than expected, perhaps reflecting a resignation that hacking—and its consequences—have come to be expected by the public. This raises the question whether cybersecurity is increasingly perceived as predictable and tolerable and accepted with a sense of resignation.

Perhaps that possible reality reflects an understanding that loss of privacy is one of the unintended consequences of the digital age in which we live. The question of privacy is discussed in the Criminal Procedure Class I course. My students largely, but not unanimously, articulate an understanding that their privacy has been minimized.

It is, for them, their reality. Perhaps this explains the following: according to my friend, an overwhelming number of clients rejected a data protection plan that the corporation offered. Not all, but most of them were rejected.

I find this particularly interesting with respect to this book project. In some ways, it captures the extraordinary complexity of technology and its intersection with the individual. The challenge is to reconcile technology's dangers with its advantages; the question is, how does the confluence between the two impact articulation and implementation of cybersecurity strategy? Doing so requires understanding the fact that cyber, in the wrong hands, poses significant dangers to individuals, corporations, states, and society alike.

There is, necessarily, a caveat: there is no foolproof protection available. Attacks will occur, and harm will be caused. In some ways, this was the gist of my conversation with the corporate executive and the reaction of his customers to the hack.

They were not surprised; he was also not surprised. However, this does not suggest that we must raise our hands in a collective *woe is me, there is nothing to do.* Our defeatism plays into the hands of those intending to do us harm. The question that will be explored in this book is as follows: What measures can be taken to minimize risks and attack impacts?

As discussed in the pages ahead, it is essential we recognize the need to undertake a profound shift in our approach to cybersecurity. Minimizing the threat—whether proactively or reactively—requires recognizing the threat and establishing cooperation and collaboration mechanism among distinct sectors and populations, regardless of whatever competing interests may suggest reluctance in joining forces.

The concept of cooperation—both in the abstract and concrete—is essential to combating cybersecurity. It is a theme that runs through this book; although repetitions can be irritating, the concept is so critical to counter effectively the threat posed by cyber attacks that it is one that we will refer to on a number of occasions.

Cybersecurity and cyberterrorism are like a mirror of each other: Cybersecurity is the response to cyberterrorism; cyberterrorism can be mitigated only by effective cybersecurity. Examining one requires discussing the other. The discussion is otherwise incomplete. However, the discussion is significantly hampered by a complicated reality: terms are ever evolving, more unsettled than settled, and more amorphous than clear.

This imposes significant burdens on law enforcement, national security officials, corporate leaders, and policy makers. The inherent fluidity of the terminology reflects an uncertainty regarding the threat posed by cyber. The nefarious use of cyber has clearly extraordinarily powerful repercussions for individuals, government, and corporations. Compounding the difficulty in confronting the threats posed by cyber is its relative *new-ness*.

While writing this book, I have been struck by an unwillingness of corporate leaders to fully recognize the threat posed by cyber. I am hard-pressed to accept the fact that the failure reflects an inability to understand; rather, I believe that the failure reflects an unwillingness to directly confront the threat posed by cyber and the burdens and responsibilities cyber imposes on corporate leadership. I find this deeply troubling, if not unconscionable.

That conviction was repeatedly reinforced in conversations with corporate officials. It is frankly a dangerous road to travel. After all, the threat is real with potentially devastating consequences. To willingly ignore—or deliberately minimize—the consequences of a potential cyber attack is akin to *playing with fire*.

Corporate leaders and government officials owe a duty: corporations to shareholders and customers, and government to citizens. This is a duty that can neither be mitigated nor derogated. Understanding the threat posed by cyber requires looking the tiger in the proverbial eye. The metaphor is not an exaggeration; harmful use of cyber is, literally, a tiger posing significant threats to contemporary society.

There is, literally, no choice. Doing so requires cooperation among distinct actors. This sounds simple and logical. However, cooperation must occur among actors naturally suspicious of each other or whose organizational DNA does not equate to cooperative efforts with others. Both realities are unfortunate.

It is unfortunately not only for corporate leaders who must be singled out. A few years ago, a sobering encounter happened at a lunch with FBI and local law enforcement officials. The FBI officials were crystal clear that cooperation with the latter was a *nonstarter*. I was stunned by the directness with which the statement was made; it goes without saying that the local officials were insulted. Whether it was the intention of the FBI officials was unclear; it is also, frankly, irrelevant. What is relevant is the content: federal-local law enforcement cooperation is problematic and challenging, to say the least.

However, effective *cybersecurity* requires that law enforcement—federal, state, and local—recognize their duty to the public, and it requires institutionalized cooperation. This is, the degree of cooperation—whether minimal or maximum—cannot be dependent on the whims and fancies of particular individuals. Devoid of a comprehensive and institutionalized approach to cybersecurity, cyber-terrorism will have the upper hand for years to come.

However, cooperation must occur beyond narrowly defined law enforcement; corporations, state agencies, and law enforcement must undertake institutionalized efforts to develop systematic and systemic approaches to mutually minimizing threats posed by cyberterrorism. A phone conversation with a local law enforcement official highlighted the challenges posed. In a very direct and candid manner, the official powerfully highlighted two critical weaknesses regarding the development of effective cybersecurity: jurisdictional *turf-fighting* between different local agencies and a lack of corporate willingness to cooperate with law enforcement. I asked for examples and he provided two, one for each paradigm. Both are distressing.

The official related that in a complex money laundering operation, two different local (neither state nor federal) law enforcement agencies, including his, failed to cooperate. When I pressed him as to know the cause, his answer was honest and troublesome: because it did not serve our interest to do so. We spoke on two different occasions; in both, he repeated the story and the explanation.

I believe he understood that the conduct of both agencies endangered the public. At some level, his answer is equivalent to the irritating phrase, *it is what it is*. Irritating? Doubtlessly. Irresponsible? Totally. Demanding profound changes? Absolutely. What struck me is the lack of overarching institutionalized authority, much less on the ground leadership, that could—literally—force cooperation. That is a powerful weakness in U.S. cyber policy.

The second story focused on corporations.

The official was unsparing in his criticism of corporate leadership. He faulted them for focusing on short-term quarterly earnings rather than long-term vulnerabilities. Although recognizing duty to shareholders is a primary obligation of corporate leaders, he rejected a *black–white* paradigm whereby corporations chose not to cooperate with law enforcement in the immediate aftermath of cyber penetration. His insistence on this matter resonated with me. I fully agreed with him.

I digress: A number of years ago, I was appointed as a legal advisor to a U.S. Congress Task Force mandated to develop national homeland security. I worked under the auspices of the House of Representatives Committee on Homeland Security. The appointment included both testifying before the Committee and submitting research papers. Given below is an excerpt from one of the papers; by analogy it is directly relevant to the question of cooperation that is of central importance to this book:

Analyzing the threat

1. What is the threat the state faces?
2. Who is responsible for planning the threat?
3. Who is responsible for financing the threat?
4. Who is responsible for carrying out the threat?
5. When will the threat likely be carried out?

Figure 1.1 Analyzing the threat.

The first step in creating an effective counterterrorism measure is analyzing the threat. To that end, the questions raised in Figure 1.1 must be answered.*

Once these questions are answered, the threat can be placed on an imminent continuum with the understanding that one large threat may be composed of smaller, more manageable, threats. The imminent continuum has four major threats as benchmarks: imminent, foreseeable, long range, and uncertain.

Imminent threats are those that are to be shortly conducted; as an example a hot intelligence report suggests that a bomb will be detonated tomorrow at 9:11 a.m. at a domestic terminal at JFK Airport.

Foreseeable threats are those that will be carried out in near future (with no specificity); therefore, they are more distant than an imminent threat. For example, a foreseeable threat would be premised on valid intelligence, indicating terrorists will shortly begin bringing explosives onto airplanes in liquid substances.

Long-range threats are threats that may reach fruition at an unknown time; for example, terrorists' training with no operational measure specifically planned would fit in this category.

Uncertain threats constitute those threats that invoke general fears of insecurity. As a result of train bombings in England and Spain, travelers in the United States might potentially or conceivably feel insecure riding trains without bolstered security. This would be true regardless of whether there is valid intelligence, indicating terrorists intend to target trains in the United States.

In determining where a particular threat fits on the imminent continuum, the balance must be struck between national security and

---

* http://papers.ssrn.com/sol3/papers.cfm?abstract_id=1090328.

competing rights interests. The following Figure 1.2 depicts the imminent continuum graphically. The threat of a terrorist attack is listed from left to right, progressing from imminent to uncertain. The vertical column on the left lists seven factors that counterterrorism measures must balance in considering these threats. The balancing factors include collateral damage, civil liberties, valid intelligence, frequency of reporting, fiscal responsibility, geopolitical concerns, and the rule of law. Understanding these factors is crucial; detailed explanations are outlined below the chart. The triangular bars in the body of the graph represent the relative priority placed on each of these factors in the event of an imminent, foreseeable, long-range, or uncertain threat of a terrorist attack. The thicker the triangular bar, the greater the importance of the corresponding factor. For example, the triangular bar representing the first factor, collateral damage, is thicker for an imminent threat and becomes thinner as it reaches an uncertain threat. This bar indicates that collateral damage is more likely for imminent counterterrorism measures than for foreseeable, long-range, or uncertain measures.

The key is to understand the significance of how balancing competing factors determines effectiveness (Figures 1.2 and 1.3).

In many ways, my conversation with the local law official was integral to my undertaking this book project. The second impetus was an invitation from the not-for-profit National Cyber Partnership to teach a course, global perspectives on cybercrime and cyberterrorism, as part of their groundbreaking, fast track training program targeting transitioning military and veterans seeking jobs in the cyber industry.

Focusing on the legal and policy aspects of cybersecurity, I sought to highlight important issues that would serve as discussion points for my four intended audiences: corporate leaders, law enforcement officials, policy makers, and the general public. No one audience is more salient or relevant than another. In many ways, all four audiences need to understand how cyber impacts both itself and the other three audiences.

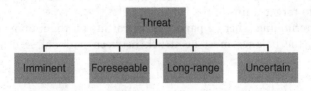

Figure 1.2 Threat characteristics.

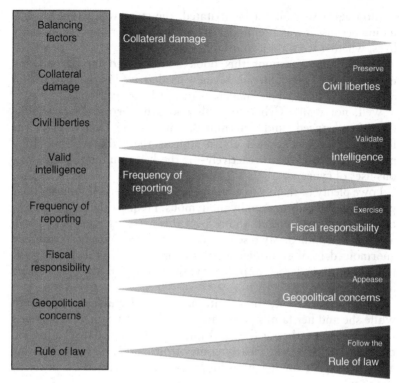

Figure 1.3 Balancing factors.

The threat posed by cybercriminals and cyberterrorism deeply affects each and every one of us. That is not intended either as an exaggeration or empty mantra.

I was reminded of that reality when an e-mail appeared in my inbox in December 2015. The sender was my credit card company. Their very effective and impressive tracking system, predicated on a sophisticated algorithm, triggered suspicion that my account had been hacked. The purchase, both content and location, did not reflect my traditional habits. The system was correct: I had never visited the location in question and had not made the purchase.

This means that the system worked. Speaking with my account manager, I expressed my gratitude for the effectiveness of their model. When we finished our conversation I was—yet again—struck by how common is the unfortunate intersection between cyber and its unintended use.

Although I was only a bit irritated, the story was telling. It was telling because it was a reminder of how much cyber impacts our daily lives, whether we want it to or not.

The broader questions this book addresses go far beyond any inconvenience I encountered. My new card arrived in the mail within a few days; I suffered no financial harm. All was well.

Well, not really. **Cybercriminals** and **cyberterrorists** are sophisticated, advanced, and determined. This is the reality. How the four audiences mentioned above address these threats—hopefully proactively, rather than reactively—is the key to minimizing nefarious uses of cyber.

I owe plenty of thanks to a number of people; at their request, their participation needs to remain anonymous. I request the reader that he or she should understand and respect this necessity. One person can and must be named: My research assistant, Stacey Wright, is owed an enormous debt of gratitude. Stacey's contribution to this book is significant at many levels, in particular the graphics in the pages ahead and in Chapter 9.

To her great credit, she maintained a wonderful sense of humor while she and her family were faced with a significant challenge. As I told Stacey's father at the SJ Quinney College of Law graduation on May 13, 2016, she clearly comes from *good stock*. She has my greatest respect for her unfailing grace. I can only say a heartfelt *thank you*.

I was determined to highlight critical issues in this book with the hope of engendering conversations among disparate audiences. To do so, an author is best—I believe—served by drawing attention to critical issues and suggesting particular ways to resolve them.

In seeking to reach distinct audiences, this book adopts a conversational tone; it is neither a classic textbook intended exclusively for academia nor a *how to* book, focusing solely on corporations and law enforcement. The intention is deliberately interdisciplinary and multidisciplinary (they are distinct terms) in order to address legal and policy aspects of cyber security.

This book is organized in such a way that it brings the complexity of cybersecurity to life. This is done through a series of vignettes, created as exercises intended to confront the reader with the dilemmas involved in cybersecurity. The vignettes, arguably, are more effective teaching examples than just text; it is a tool to bring the issue to life. Important to add is that the vignettes are also applicable to corporate audiences, whether the C level or the less senior executives.

Similarly, it is my hope that law enforcement—local, state, and national in the United States and their relevant counterparts in other countries—will find the vignettes relevant in their continuing efforts to better understand cybersecurity in an effort to improve their abilities to minimize its nefarious impacts. Finally, I hope that the general public will find the discussion and vignettes useful in enhancing their understanding of this significant threat.

The vignettes highlight the constant threat of cybersecurity and the fast-pace evolution of the threat against the various audiences. The imminence of cybersecurity is rapidly evolving with so much uncertainty. Thus, the vignettes are intended to facilitate discussion and reaction to actual, probable events. In addition, the vignettes are to be used to prompt conversation among individuals, business associates, and law enforcement and government agencies.

In this spirit, Chapter 8 is composed primarily of vignettes. This is deliberate. This is meant to force application and process as the reader confronts what was written in the previous chapters and how to apply it in real-life scenarios.

Overall, the purpose of the vignettes is to highlight the complexity of cybersecurity, facilitate discussion, and hopefully lead to resolution of many open-ended issues. The vignettes are relevant to the four distinct audiences: corporate leaders, academia, law enforcement, and the general public.

In this spirit, it is my hope that the proposals suggested in this book will be viewed as recommended *best practices*. The word *recommended* is deliberately chosen: given the complexity attendant to cyber, if a particular proposal or discussion point contributes to resolving a particular conundrum, then my purpose of writing this book will be achieved.

It is, therefore, my intention that the reader will view the discussion points as intended to facilitate candid and frank examination of a threat directed at individuals, corporations, and government. To facilitate this discussion, this book is divided as follows.

CHAPTER TWO: WHAT IS CYBERSECURITY?

Definitions are essential to creating and implementing a cyber policy predicated on the rule of law. To that end, **cybersecurity** is the effort to protect information, communications, and technology from the harm caused either accidentally or intentionally; it is important to emphasize that a cyber attack is profoundly distinct from a physical attack. Further, cybersecurity is the effort to ensure the confidentiality, integrity, and availability of data, resources, and processes through the use of administrative, physical, and technical controls.

CHAPTER THREE: GEOPOLITICS AND CYBERSECURITY

In this chapter, the relationship between cybersecurity and **geopolitics** will be examined by analyzing particular examples reflecting the complexity of their confluence. The analysis will touch upon international law, specifically self-defense and proportionality. Nation-state decision making, reflecting predictability and consistency, significantly enhances global order. However, threats—whether actual or perceived—dramatically impact regional and global stability. In this vein, assessing how nation-states respond, whether unilaterally, bilaterally, or multilaterally, to particular crisis points is essential to understanding the practical impact of geopolitical considerations.

CHAPTER FOUR: INTERNATIONAL LAW AND CYBERSECURITY BACKGROUND

An important question to ask is whether or not the law applies to cybersecurity, and if the law applies to cybersecurity, what are the relevant legal structures?

How the nation-state responds to a cyber attack reflects the essence of international law, predicated on the nation-state's right to defend itself—when attacked—in accordance with Article 51 of the UN Charter.

CHAPTER FIVE: DEVELOPMENT AND IMPLEMENTATION OF CYBERSECURITY POLICY

In this chapter, the focus will be on the development and implementation of cybersecurity *policy*. Policy requires a thorough, interdisciplinary analysis of the issue in order to develop the most effective responses to the threat posed by cyber attacks.

CHAPTER SIX: HOW DO CORPORATIONS RESPOND TO CYBERCRIME?

Corporations large and small are subject to hackers and are clearly being attacked, if not on a daily basis, but very regularly. Some of the attacks are enormous, affecting tens of millions of customers whose privacy is clearly violated. Their personal information is hacked; they are vulnerable, exposed, and concerned, if not angry. How corporations respond to cybersecurity is critical. The extraordinary importance cuts across tactical and strategic considerations. It is not an exaggeration to suggest that cyber threats are the primary focal point of corporations today. If they are not, then that reflects a serious misreading of a clear and present danger. That danger—palpable to the most casual observer—is indisputable.

CHAPTER SEVEN: HOW CAN INDIVIDUALS MITIGATE CYBERSECURITY?

Moving on from corporations, we can next consider who makes up corporations. Individuals can mitigate the threats, dangers, and vulnerabilities posed by cybersecurity. Each of us, individually, plays a role in the context of cybersecurity. Here is a small example. Many of us have been hacked, whether our credit card is breached, or our e-mail is hacked. Thus, each one of us has personal experience. Cybersecurity can be viewed at both personal and broad levels.

CHAPTER EIGHT: HOW DOES LAW ENFORCEMENT MITIGATE CYBERSECURITY?

This chapter discusses the relationship between law enforcement and cybersecurity, specifically how law enforcement can more effectively work with corporations, individuals, and states to assist them in protecting from cyber attacks. The emphasis will be on what law enforcement can do to mitigate cybersecurity or cyber threats.

CHAPTER NINE: CYBERSECURITY IN THE FUTURE

This chapter emphasizes cybersecurity in the future, the enormity of the risk, and the steps to be taken to mitigate that risk. The use of various scenarios will make the conversation more realistic and less theoretical. This is done to help the reader understand cybersecurity at its most practical level.

CHAPTER TEN: FINAL WORD

In the preceding pages, a number of issues relevant to cybersecurity have been raised with a particular focus on legal and policy questions. Although technical questions are of the utmost importance, they were not the focus. The larger question, and hence the title "final word," is where do we go from here? Perhaps, more than anything else, this is the critical point of inquiry for the reader and author.

2 What is cybersecurity?

INTRODUCTION

The question posed in this chapter's title is the subject of endless discussion, conjecture, and writing. The term is much discussed, causing great anxiety and posing more questions than answers. Experts and nonexperts alike articulate concern reflecting vulnerability, a sense that their privacy is *at risk* and that *unseen* forces are at bay. Minimized privacy is the reality of the modern, technology-driven and -based age. The question in the context of cybersecurity is as follows: Whether minimization poses threats, endangering individuals and society alike? The common assumption suggests that the answer is in *affirmative*.

However, it is similarly the case that modern technology has enormous benefits that have, without doubt, dramatically impacted, if not improved, our lives. Examples are bountiful and familiar to all, ranging from the mundane to the complex. In many ways, we all benefit from living in the technology age. However, those benefits are, unfortunately, tempered by negative consequences emanating from the misuse—primarily deliberate—of technology.

This misuse is the focus of this book; focusing on the negative use of technology facilitates a discussion regarding how society and individuals can more effectively establish protection mechanisms. Doing so requires acknowledging that danger emanating from nefarious application of technology demands our individual and their collective attention.

In the course of researching and writing this book, it was suggested to me that the cyber threat is exaggerated, and that cybersecurity reflects a cottage industry gone awry. Although reasonable minds can disagree, I find that perspective to be incorrect. A casual glance at headlines unequivocally suggests that the threat is neither negligible nor passing. Quite the opposite.

To what extent it endangers depends on what, and when, protective measures are undertaken. This is a double-edged sword: Protection is justified if the source of danger is properly identified. However, rashly acting against a perceived or potential threat raises troubling questions regarding preemptive and disproportionate application of state power. Akin to traditional threats and dangers, an effort to mitigate potential danger is subject to restrictions imposed by domestic and international laws.

Transitioning from traditional warfare to cyberterrorism and **cyber warfare** reflects a significant change in the nature of conflict and modes and manners of defense. If traditional warfare between nation-states involved tanks, planes, and ships, then cyber attacks, whether conducted by nation-states or nonstate actors, require a laptop and computer sophistication and savvy.

Cyber attacks address nation-state infrastructure but can also address infrastructure moving forward. As will be discussed in the pages ahead, preventing and reacting to a cyber attack poses significant challenges to the nation-state.

Cyber—incorporating cybersecurity, cyberterrorism, and cyber attacks—reflects the cutting edge of technology. Ten, much less twenty years ago, this conversation would have been viewed largely as futuristic. The morph from traditional warfare to conventional terrorism and to cyber reflects a significant change in how conflict is conducted. From the perspective of decision makers, this transition is dramatic; from the perspective of the public, cyber attacks are a source of enormous concern and discomfort.

Conflict, both presently and in the years ahead, will primarily focus on nonstate actors engaged with state actors. This is the essence of terrorism as manifested in a long litany of attacks conducted against the nation-state and innocent civilians. The cyber capabilities of nonstate and state actors impose a burden on the nation-state's organs—military, the intelligence community, and law enforcement—to create sophisticated defensive and offensive countermeasures. Those responses are best described as cybersecurity.

DEFINITIONS AND IMPACTS

Definitions are essential to creating and implementing a cyber policy predicated on the rule of law. To that end, **cybersecurity** is the effort to protect information, communications, and technology from harm caused either accidentally or intentionally; important to emphasize is that a cyber attack is profoundly distinct from a physical attack. Further, cybersecurity is the effort to ensure the confidentiality, integrity, and availability of data, resources, and processes through the use of administrative, physical, and technical controls.

A **cyber attack** is a deliberate and direct aggressive action intended to harm critical infrastructure. Further, a cyber attack is any deliberate attempt to compromise the confidentiality, integrity, or availability of data, resources, or processes through the use of electronic means. Obvious targets range from city's water system or transportation system to an individual's bank or credit card account. Although the hacking of a personal bank account is doubtlessly irritating, the impact of a cyber attack on a municipal water system or air traffic infrastructure can cause mayhem, extending significantly beyond an act of conventional terrorism regardless of the fact that its visceral impact is significantly different.

For example, a number of years ago, I met with a senior vice president of a leading U.S. financial institution who shared that a terrorist organization had successfully hacked sophisticated firewalls and created over 400 fictitious accounts using the same number of fictitious social security numbers. As a result of that very successful hacking, the group was able to illegally wire hundreds of millions of dollar from the United States to the Middle East through a number of different countries. The incident highlights that one cyber attack can, in the long run, have significantly greater strategic impact, than a specific act of traditional terrorism resulting in the loss of innocent life.

Cybersecurity is intended to protect society and individuals from very sophisticated and aggressive attacks; the important question is determining the prioritization of what we seek to protect. The answer is extremely complicated because prioritization requires answering a series of questions, including those given in Figure 2.1.

- To what extent is the state required to protect civilians?
- To what extent is the state required to protect public infrastructure?
- To what extent is the state required to protect overseas assets, public and private?

Figure 2.1 Prioritization questions.

VIGNETTE

With cybersecurity being the protection of information, communications, and technology from harm, and cyber attack being defined as a deliberate and direct aggressive action intended to harm critical infrastructure, each subset of those definitions must be broken down in determining whether a cyber attack has taken place, and whether cybersecurity is implicated.

First, consider the following example: An individual accesses his or her bank account and realizes that the money has disappeared. Not only that, he or she receives collection letters and calls from agencies claiming they owe large amounts of money in various cities. This individual is a victim of identity theft. Identity theft is the misuse of an individual's social security number. Does that fit within the definition of cybersecurity—with it being the protection of information, communications, and technology from harm? Absolutely. The misuse of one's social security number deals with the lack of protection of information from harm.

Does that experience fit within the definition of a cyber attack— with it being a direct and deliberate aggressive action intended to harm critical infrastructure? Critical infrastructure is the operative word in this analysis. There is no doubt that stealing one's personal information, particularly their social security number, is a direct and deliberate aggressive action intended to harm that individual. But, does that individual fit within the definition of critical infrastructure? That will be discussed in later chapters.

Second, consider the following example. An individual goes to turn on the shower to get ready for work and, alas, no water. The individual knows they have paid their bill, and water should be flowing, however it is not. Come to find out—an organization has breached the computers at the local water station—stopping all water access to the community. Does that fit within the definition of cybersecurity—with it being the protection of information, communications, and technology from harm? Absolutely. The misuse of the water system in stopping water deals with the lack of protection of communication and technology from harm.

(Continued)

Does that experience fit within the definition of a cyber attack—focusing on the aspect of the definition dealing with critical infrastructure? Absolutely. Cutting off a community's access to water is without a doubt a direct and deliberate aggressive action intended to harm the critical infrastructure of the community: its supply of water. Thus, this example is easier to fit into the realm of a cybersecurity breach as a victim of a cyber attack.

As seen above with the two examples, it is difficult to ascertain whether cybersecurity has been breached and whether it suffices as a cyber attack. However, what is not difficult to ascertain is how magnificent the impact of a cyber attack can be, and how quickly it can affect a great number of individuals.

The easy answer is that the fundamental duty of the nation-state is to protect its innocent civilian population from direct harm. This is exactly why cybersecurity is so complicated because a cyber attack need not necessarily be a direct attack. Although the hacking of my credit card account was a direct attack (on me), the possibility a municipal water system will be attacked requires city, state, and federal officials to evaluate the impact on multiple levels of a cyber attack. In the context of priorities and prioritization, cybersecurity requires reprioritization of already limited resources. Cybersecurity is complicated not only in the extent of the attack but also the long-term damages that could be caused by such attacks.

To make the point clear: Cyber attacks, although distinct from physical terrorism, bring terrorism to the nation's front door. Rather than engaging terrorists in Pakistan, Syria, and Yemen, cyber vulnerability is reflected in attacks on valuable domestic assets. The reality of a cyber attack is that the person responsible for the attack can physically be as close as across the street, sitting next to you in a coffee house, or thousands of miles away. In addition, cyber attacks permeate far beyond the Internet that we now understand, as far as our capabilities and impact on everyday life.

That person has at his or her availability a computer system, or a laptop, iPhone, or iPad, enabling him or her to hack into personal databases or a city's water system. Unlike conventional terrorism, which requires a physical act of violence, a cyber attack requires everyday machinery and requisite technical skills. The combination of a computer and a skilled cyber attack accentuates the individual and collective vulnerability distinct from a conventional attack. Cyber attacks are clearly used to send a message, seen as a *diplomacy of messages*. This message specifically affects the psychology of vulnerability, the trust and confidence people have in combating such attacks. One of the primary differences is that a terrorist conducting a traditional attack can be seen, whereas those responsible for a cyber attack are largely invisible. The difference between the two raises profound questions regarding vulnerability and protection.

TERRORISM

Although there are, literally, an endless number of definitions of terrorism, I suggest **terrorism** be defined as an act, by an individual or a group, intended to kill innocent individuals, primarily as a way of instilling fear in others, with the purpose of advancing one of four causes—political, religious, social, and cultural—with respect to government policy. The overwhelming majority of terrorist attacks result in the random loss of innocent life; however, from the perspective of terrorist organizations, the civilian population is defined as legitimate targets. However, cybersecurity is very different for people who are not being killed or physically injured. However, the long-term impact of a cyber attack is more powerful than a single act of terrorism. Cyber terrorism reflects a profoundly different skill set and approach; whereas the traditional terrorist was willing to die for *the cause*, the cyber attacker is not physically engaged and is, therefore, not risking life or limb. However, the cyber attacker can drastically impact everyday life, in a more impactful way than traditional terrorism. Although both traditional terrorists and cyber attackers are deeply devoted to their cause, the terrorist manipulating a computer does not intend to die while committing his act.

Arguably that makes him more dangerous: because of their computer sophistication and analytical skills, their impact on the nation-state's infrastructure extends far beyond that of a suicide bomber. In this context, one of the important questions is as follows: Whether sufficient means have been taken to protect society against what is, in essence, a new form of terrorism? One of the most important questions is the *cost* question; rearticulated, how expensive it is to implement countercyber measures. Doubtlessly it is very expensive, primarily because it requires responding in a sophisticated manner to sophisticated attacks. Given the, literally, unlimited definitions of *legitimate target*, the consequences in the context of a cyber attack are staggering: the successful penetration of a commercial airliner or of an airport system has the potential for an extraordinary terrorist attack. The consequences of harm, short and long term alike, dramatically extend beyond traditional terrorism.

VIGNETTE

The impact of a cyber attack on a nation-state is significant. Not only it is a significant threat to a nation-state's infrastructure, but the ability to protect against it comes at an enormous cost. As the cost often outweighs the threat, many points of critical infrastructure are left vulnerable. This leaves us with the question—what would I do in such an attack?

Consider your morning routine—what is one of the first things you do in the morning? Typically, you would wake up, rise from your bed, and flip on the lights. But, what if you could not flip on the lights? In addition, what if all the food in your refrigerator gets spoiled due to lack of electricity? This is a situation that occurred recently in Ukraine, which was said to be at the hands of a cyber attack. A region in Ukraine went dark for three hours, but not due to some "rusty connection or a tree falling on a power line but appeared to be a rare example of malware being used to switch off an electrical grid."* This example of a cyber attack clearly demonstrates the instability that can be caused by cyber terrorism. In addition, it leads to the conclusion that not only could a malware shut down the power grid, a similar kind could "manipulate machines that control industrial equipment" and "cause them to behave in dangerous ways."† With that example—does the cost still outweigh the threat?

---

* https://www.washingtonpost.com/opinions/a-cautionary-blackout-in-ukraine/2016/02/17/da2d58ac-b4c5-11e5-9388-466021d971de_story.html?wpmm=1&wpisrc=nl_opinions.
† *Id.*

COST

How much money should be allocated to cybersecurity? In addition, how much damage can a cyber attack cause? And finally, more importantly, how much damage are we willing to tolerate? To begin the process of answering these questions, it is important to recognize that the transition from the conventional terrorism or counterterrorism model is going to require a fundamental rearticulation of defining threat, and what and who poses a threat. The current U.S. operational counterterrorism model is primarily predicated on drone attacks against suspected terrorist targets.

Whether that model is legal, moral, and effective is the most important point of inquiry. However, because the threat posed by cyber is different from that posed by a potential suicide bomber, reformulating operational counterterrorism is essential. If drone warfare is the weapon of choice with respect to conventional terrorism, then preventing or responding to a cyber attack is very different primarily because the cyber attacker is not readily visible. The distinction in physicality requires rethinking both our basic understanding of terrorism and reformulating counterterrorism to respond to the cyber threat. In addition, it requires rethinking what become targets during cyber attacks, specifically considering the infrastructure that is most critical to protect.

One of the important questions is to determine whether individuals involved in cyber terrorism are **legitimate targets**, akin to those involved in conventional terrorism. I would suggest the following: an individual involved in cyber terrorism, who has the ability to hack into a city's water system, is a legitimate target as is the terrorist who intends to commit a suicide bombing. The rationale for this *equivalency* is the potential for harm they pose and the actual harm they may cause.

The overwhelming importance of intelligence information cannot be minimized. Similar to conventional terrorism, the decision whether to target an individual involved in cyber terrorism will be determined by the analysis of relevant intelligence information. Both in conventional terrorism and cyber terrorism, the intelligence community is composed of two distinct branches: information gathering and information analysis. However, because cyber is a new form of warfare, there is a requirement to rethink the traditional intelligence-gathering model.

The difference is stark: cyber is predicated on an individual holding a laptop with no intention of dying, whereas the suicide bomber intends to die while committing an act of terrorism. Although both individuals pose a threat to national security, the difference in their abilities, means, and consequences are significant.

VIGNETTE

Cyberterrorism differs from traditional terrorism, as predicated earlier, most specifically by the individual instigating the attack. The cyber terrorist is often an individual holding a laptop with no intention of dying. He is not readily identifiable. This plays directly into the cost question. Consider the following:

In furtherance of our earlier example, an individual wakes up and turns on the water tap for a morning shower and then finds no water. The individual learns that a cyber attack has been carried out against the community's water system, with the computers breached, and all access to water has been cut off. As discussed previously, this constitutes a cyber attack because it is a direct and deliberate aggressive action and it deals with harm against technology and communications.

The question then becomes, how significant is the attack? Often, the significance of the attack affects our cost analysis. The pinnacle question raised at the beginning of this section is how much money should be allocated to cybersecurity? Imagine you are that individual living in the community with a sudden scarcity of water. Forget the desire for good hygiene; suddenly, your food options are significantly limited. Not only that, even if you are able to cook, your ability to wash the dishes for reuse is hindered due to the lack of water. In addition, you are unable to use your toilet. Without running water, our daily existence ceases to become normal and would likely revert into a chaotic sense.

Thus, with the question being how significant is the attack, how would you rate the lack of running water? Would that be a 10 on the significance scale? Is it as significant as a terrorist bombing in a nearby hotel? Is the threat just as real? Is it more or less likely to impact your daily life? The lack of running water not only to an individual but also to businesses, or a hospital system, is a threat that has great significance.

(Continued)

It would seem that the allocation of money should be an easy question. However, the follow-up questions introduce difficulties into the scenario. How much damage can a cyber attack cause? As seen in this example, the amount of damage is significant. Without running water, society as we know it is unable to function. Thus, the amount of damage a cyber attack can cause is great. Although the damage is not physical, and may not be immediately visible to the human eye, it seems to be greater than the more traditional forms of terrorism due to its widespread nature and the amount of individuals it will affect.

The final follow-up question asks how much damage are we willing to tolerate? This cost question is difficult to answer, specifically, because the amount of damage we are willing to tolerate often plays off the amount of damage we have experienced, and vow to never experience again. Until a cyber attack occurs, many discount the threat, or see it as unlikely or not feasible. However, once such an attack occurs, as seen in a previous example, with the lights going out in portions of Ukraine, the amount of damage a group is willing to tolerate greatly decreases. Thus, it is critical to get ahead of the cost question to effectively combat the effects of a cyber attack.

ACTS OF TERRORISM

A successful **suicide bombing** requires somewhere four to five distinct actors: the cell leader; the person responsible for logistics; the financier; the bomber; and the person who creates the environment contributing to the legitimacy of suicide bombing. Subject to the extent and timing of their individual involvement, all five are legitimate targets. The question is, *when* are they legitimate targets? In contrast, cybersecurity does not require similar infrastructure for a successful attack on a municipality's water system. Rather, all that may be needed is a computer savvy individual with a laptop and the ability to hack into that specific city's water system.

A suicide bombing requires four or five distinct actors working together, creating a cell, planning a sophisticated operation; conversely, a cyber attack requires one individual who in all likelihood will not be killed or die while engaging in hacking.

The threat posed by cyber requires an intelligence gathering and analysis model different from conventional terrorism. Similarly, the cyber protection model is distinct from the model intended to protect the nation-state from conventional terrorism. The primary reason for the distinction is predicated on the requirement to create sophisticated firewalls intended to protect computer systems. This is distinct from, and more complex than, protecting buildings and other physical locations.

The reality of cybersecurity is that it poses burdens, obligations, and responsibilities on government and corporations that significantly differ from traditional asset protection models. The conventional protection model is predicated on manpower intensive *force protection* in response to a specific risk assessment and cost–benefit analysis. In the traditional model, soldiers protect bases, policemen protect buildings, and law enforcement protects individuals. Cybersecurity and cyber attacks are totally different: although physical damage may be incurred, the impetus for the attack is the hacking into a **computer network**.

The physical attack that is the essence of conventional terrorism has increasingly given way to terrorism, whereby systems will be attacked; therefore, the primary effort is to secure digital information. That is not to minimize nor negate the possible physical danger and harm that result from a cyber attack; however, at its essence, a cyber attack is profoundly different from a traditional attack. At its essence, the danger posed by a cyber attack is that the core infrastructure systems will be impacted; the possible consequences are staggering. The effort to secure extraordinary complicated and complex digital information is expensive, daunting, and essential. The cost of cyber defense is astronomical and varies depending on the circumstances.

The failure to secure digital information will have dramatic consequences: loss of privacy, enhanced vulnerability, significant financial impact, and the underlying fear that emanates from the *unseen* enemy.

Conventional terrorism can be described as the danger posed by the *unseen enemy in the back alley*, which explicitly suggests a physical threat. Conversely, cybersecurity is an attack on the intangible, an attack by the unseen on the unseen. Effectively addressing this threat requires both implementing a fundamental rearticulation of the intelligence model to better understand the threat and an enhanced understanding of our individual and collective vulnerability. In stark terms, the laptop is, in essence, the mechanism or conduit by which terrorists attack. Opening our laptops and entering our passwords require asking whether sufficient protection measures have been undertaken.

VIGNETTE

In considering the traditional form of terrorism, involving four to five distinct actors, the cost of such an effort is great, specifically in terms of a cyber attack involving one individual. The four to five distinct actors in traditional terrorism consist of (1) **the cell leader; (2) the person responsible for logistics;** (3) **the financier;** (4) **the bomber; and the** (5) **person who creates the environment contributing to the legitimacy of suicide bombing.** Each individual comes at a cost. The cell leader requires money to engage and attract other members to join their cause. The person responsible for logistics needs money to fund the operation, including the purchase of cell phones, weapons, investigative resources, and cars.

The financier is the financial supporter of the operation. Ultimately, in traditional terrorism, their goal is to make the greatest statement, and often the greater the statement the greater the cost. It is the financier's job to acquire the money to fund the operation. In addition, the bomber comes at the greatest cost. Although bombers are likely not paid for their services because they will not likely live past the operation, there is significant money that goes in seducing the individual to play the role of a bomber. And finally, the person creating the environment contributing to the legitimacy of suicide bombing requires money to create such an environment to make the greatest statement.

The discussion of money plays a critical role in traditional terrorism. The four to five individuals playing a role in the act, and the money required to make such an act occur, creates several opportunities for counterterrorist groups to learn of such an attack and thwart its success. Without money or communications, a counterterrorist unit can stop the progression of a conventional terrorist attack. Thus, the usage of more individuals and need for money create greater penetration points for counterterrorist intelligence to halt the operation.

On the contrary, cyber attack has significantly less penetration points and requires a greater upfront cost in protection to thwart an attack. Unlike conventional terrorism, cyber attack can involve only one individual. Thus, there are fewer opportunities to

(Continued)

penetrate the cell and thwart the attack. In addition, the money that flows through individuals for a conventional terrorist attack does not happen with a cyber attack, thus creating even fewer penetration points.

A singular individual can create a cyber attack against critical infrastructure, causing damage to a city's water system, flight control towers, or financial information. Owing to the individual nature, there are overall less penetration points or opportunities to thwart an operation. Thus, it comes at a greater cost, and one that is often dismissed. It is easy to convince someone to pay for protection against a physical attack—the damage is indisputable and one the public can immediately understand. On the other hand, a cyber threat, although just as significant, if not arguably more significant, is more dismissive and difficult to imagine; therefore, the demand for adequate protection is oft ignored.

As mentioned earlier, the ability to hop online, enter your password, and access your bank account information is a great tool to aid to the efficiency of our day-to-day activities. However, the ability to do so must be coupled with adequate protection against cyber attackers. This protection is not adequate at this time.

HACKING

Recent cases, including the hacking of Sony Pictures* or the alleged hacking into the U.S. Central Command (CENTCOM) social media, are but examples of successful and much publicized cyber attacks. Whether it is as dramatic and consequential as the creation of 400 fictitious accounts depends on perspectives and interests; doubtlessly, all three highlight the requirement to rearticulate the traditional protection model. However, an important caveat is in order: the nation-state cannot do everything necessary to protect us. There are, after all, limits on state powers; failure to impose limits would doubtlessly and significantly violate individual rights. A democracy must find the appropriate balance between protection and individual rights.

---

* http://www.pocket-lint.com/news/131937-sony-pictures-hack-here-s-everything-we-know-about-the-massive-attack-so-far, last viewed June 1, 2015.

- Who is the actor responsible for cyber attack?
- To what extent do we want our privacy violated?
- Are individuals willing to have their privacy limited in the name of protecting themselves and others?

Figure 2.2 Individual questions.

So in that context, it is important to ask the questions raised in Figure 2.2.

The instinctual response, particularly in the aftermath of 9/11 and the culture it has created, suggests a willingness to tolerate imposition on individual privacy in the name of collective and individual protection. There is, of course, great danger in advocating, much less creating, mechanisms whereby individual rights are significantly minimized. Understandable history perhaps suggests that such an approach is laden with danger and risk because the consequences of enabling significant government surveillance power can have troubling ramifications for individuals and society alike. Simply put: Once power is granted to government, reclaiming is the most difficult task and burden.

Did we agree that our privacy be unnecessarily violated? The answer is that history shows that in the immediate aftermath of a terrorist attack, we are only too happy to violate the rights of others. The question is, whether minimizing individual rights is effective in the context of cybersecurity and what is the most appropriate model for protecting individuals and society? The answer depends on how much privacy individuals are willing to sacrifice in the name of cyber protection. In the past few years there has been significant criticism of the National Security Agency (NSA) for monitoring a staggering number of phone conversations[*]; on May 7, 2015, the U.S. Court of Appeals for the Second Circuit ruled that NSA practice of collecting data about phone calls goes beyond Congressional authorization with respect to Section 215 of the **Patriot Act.**[†]

---

[*] http://www.wsj.com/articles/surveillance-court-judge-criticized-nsa-overcollection-of-data-1407806807, last viewed June 1, 2015; http://www.reuters.com/article/2015/05/07/us-usa-security-nsa-idUSKBN0NS1IN20150507, last viewed June 1, 2015.

[†] http://pdfserver.amlaw.com/nlj/NSA_ca2_20150507.pdf, last viewed June 1, 2015.

VIGNETTE

Privacy, as mentioned earlier, is a difficult conversation evolving from cyber conversations. As also mentioned earlier, in the aftermath of an attack, individuals are more likely, and more willing, to violate the rights of those involved. However, in a recent scenario, the situation has not played out as such.

On December 2, 2015, Syed Rizwan Farook and Tashfeen Malik conducted a mass shooting and attempted bombing at a work holiday party. From this attack, 14 people were killed and 22 were seriously injured. The privacy battle that stems from this attack involves access to Farook's iPhone. The FBI was unable to unlock the mobile phone and requested Apple to create a new version of the operating system that could be installed to disable certain security features. Apple initially declined, which resulted in the FBI seeking a court order, mandating Apple to create and provide the requested software. Apple has opposed their order, emphasizing the security risks that the creation of a backdoor would pose to their customers.

The relationship between corporate interests and national security are the core of the current tension between Apple and the FBI. Addressing, much less resolving, this tension is challenging. It is also essential. Respecting one must not come at the expense of the other. The U.S. District Court (Central California) order that Apple should create a *backdoor* is but the initial volley in what appears to be a prolonged legal battle. It cannot be predicted how the legal battle will be resolved.

Final outcome notwithstanding, battle lines have been drawn. Apple argues the FBI is engaged in *overreach*; the Department of Justice asserts information stored in the cell phone is vitally needed to protect the public. Both sides make a compelling argument. The discussion, however, goes beyond the question presently before the courts. The more profound strategic issue is private sector–government cooperation regarding homeland security and counterterrorism.

The questions are numerous and complex:

- If a corporation is the target of a terrorist attack, does government owe an obligation to respond in the name of national security?

(Continued)

- Is there a duty owed to shareholders in a publicly traded company or to investors and owners in a privately held corporation?
- Is an attack on an American corporation akin to an attack on the U.S. government?
- What is the relationship between economic impact and national security?

Answering these questions—or at least seeking to frame them—requires acknowledging the fact that terrorism poses a direct threat to corporate entities. Whether the terrorist threat is kinetic or cyber is irrelevant. The former suggests loss of life and physical damage; examples abound of the latter are strategic, economic, and have long-term impact.

Cyber attacks require corporations from partnerships with customers and law enforcement. That partnership is, admittedly, burdensome; the burden is simultaneously existential and practical. For law enforcement to be able to effectively protect corporations, it requires a fundamental change in the context and concept of cooperation. It will require corporations to be more forthcoming to law enforcement.

This can only occur if corporations are much more forthcoming. In that sense, the burden is on them. The failure to work hand-in-hand with law enforcement prevents development—much less implementation—of a sophisticated, corporate-law enforcement cooperation model.

However, the condition to this approach is the willingness of corporations to view law enforcement as full partners, both pre-emptively and reactively. To that end, a corporate governance model for cybersecurity is required; although presently untapped, the burden on its development rests with corporations.

Self-defense is a critical question in the cyber discussion. The inquiry is whether the nation-state owes a duty to corporations and individuals who have been victimized by a cyber attack. It is not an abstract question, but one rather intended as a concrete query.

The answers are unclear. Although an easy answer is *yes*, it is far more complicated than that. Similarly *no* is an unacceptable response because national interests do justify state involvement in cybersecurity, even when state targets are not directly attacked. Balance is hard to define and undoubtedly difficult to apply. In the context of state obligation to corporations and individuals, it would be an impractical *stretch* to impose on government, the obligation to respond to every cyber attack. That suggestion is a nonstarter from the beginning. Conversely, suggesting that government owes no duty violates the social contract that is the underpinning of civil society. That, too, is a *nonstarter*.

There are great risks in imposing *response* burdens on the nation-state in the aftermath of a cyber attack. If the attack can be traced back to state agents of another country, then legitimate questions arise regarding the limits of sovereignty, self-defense, and conflict.

These issues represent where the rubber *hits the road*. Until national leaders and corporate officers truly confront the extraordinary threats posed by cyberterrorism, we, individually and collectively, will continue to be vulnerable and *at risk*.

The Apple–FBI conflict highlights important concerns; we must take advantage of the spotlight focused on these issues and seek implementable answers to the questions posed.

LIMITS OF PROTECTION

With respect to cyber protection the question is how *effective* and *legal* are to be defined, much less implemented. The question of legality requires focusing on the 4th Amendment of the U.S. Constitution; with respect to effectiveness, the easy answer is if there has been no act of terrorism, then yes it is effective. Particular attention needs to be paid to three critical concepts: (1) necessity, (2) effectiveness, and (3) legality.

The threat posed by cyber demands the following to be protected (Figure 2.3):

- Individuals (citizens and non citizens alike) from external and internal threats
- Property: physical and intangible
- Infrastructure

Figure 2.3 Protection demands.

The extent to that protection is still being determined. Damage caused by cyber attacks to intellectual or intangible property is obviously enormous; one of the most important questions in the context of cybersecurity is how do we more effectively protect that intellectual or intangible property. Corporations focused on protecting their entity or trade secrets expend significant resources doing so. To what extent are they effective or ineffective is an open question. Even those intent on protecting their intellectual or intangible property must understand that protection is not 100% foolproof because attacks can, and will, occur. After all, hackers are constantly engaged in penetrating existing firewalls.

Protecting roadways, byways, water systems, airports, and so on comes at a significant cost; determining priorities requires risk assessment, sophisticated cost–benefit analysis, and resource allocation decision making. The process is complicated because governments have failed to candidly educate the public regarding the cost of protecting infrastructure from cyber attacks. The process is in addition complicated due to the technology each government can access. Different countries have the capability to defend differently depending on the technology and cost.

FORCE: IS A CYBER ATTACK AKIN TO THE ACT OF FORCE?

In discussing the relationship between cybersecurity and force perhaps we need to use "force" in quotations, as it is an implied or indirect force akin to an intellectual or intangible force. Figure 2.4 is a suggested checklist in analyzing force in the context of a cyber attack.

For example, the hacking of the Pentagon has clear ramifications and implications for America's national security. Similarly, an attack

---

- What is the *severity* of the force in the context of a cyber attack?
- How *immediate* is the threat?
- How *direct* is the force?
- What is the degree of *invasiveness*?
- How is force *measured*?
- Was the force *legitimate*?
- To what extent did the force *impact*?

Figure 2.4 Force analysis.

on a corporation whereby the accounts of millions of individuals are hacked and medical and financial records are leaked is an example of a severe cyber attack.

With respect to immediacy: If 70 million people have been impacted because of an attack on a major corporation, as seen in the Target breach recently, there is obviously a sense of immediacy as hackers have access to customer records that will require the impacted corporation to take immediate measures to minimize the harm and impact.

Acting immediately, and effectively, requires proactive planning ensuring a response plan intended to minimize the impact was developed in advance. That imposes, obviously, costs on corporations and government to have a plan in place to react immediately.

The next point is directness. In all three levels, the Pentagon being hacked, major corporations being impacted, and individual's account being hacked, there's a sense of directness. In all three instances, the impact is not *down the road* but clear now. In the same way, a physical attack has an immediate impact; the hacking of a bank account also has a clear immediacy. The immediacy and directness are mitigated by the extent of severity.

Next, it is important to consider the extent of invasiveness: If an individual's bank account has been hacked and consequently a credit card is being used (misused), there is clearly a sense of invasiveness. If the Pentagon has been hacked, there is a need for experts to determine the extent of the invasiveness. It is important to note that severity, immediacy, and directness do not immediately translate into invasiveness. The same is true with respect to corporations. An appropriate response requires assessing the degree to which the hack has invaded; as invasiveness is measurable, it is extremely important for corporations and government to determine the damage caused. For corporations, it is extremely important, in terms of compliance, to be forthcoming in articulating the extent of the impact and invasiveness. Articulating a measurable will be significantly enhanced by creating a matrix.

That matrix must reflect different layers of invasiveness, and it will also enable the corporation to determine to what extent their preplanning was effective or ineffective. One of the most important requirements is implementing a measurability matrix that ensures concrete determination of the impact. In the context of legitimacy and responsibility, the corporation owes primary responsibility to its clients and shareholders, whereas government owes responsibility to the public. In terms of cybersecurity, it is essential that corporations and governments institute preemptive mechanisms that enable monitoring of attempted penetrations, regardless of their costs.

The final point is asking whether some level of damage is tolerable. The reality is that even if a corporation has a sophisticated protection plan in place, it is inevitable, or all but inevitable, that there will be attempted attacks, some of which will be successful. It is critical that corporations, the government, and individuals do the following (Figure 2.5).

The following are the questions to consider in reviewing Chapter 2 (Figure 2.6).

- Create a protection plan;
- Engage in constant monitoring;
- When an attempted, or successful, hack is identified the target (corporation or government) must immediately attempt to identify the source, minimize the impact, and engage in information sharing with shareholders, law enforcement, and other corporations.

Figure 2.5 Protection plan.

- How do we measure force in cybersecurity attacks?
- What level of harm constitutes a cybersecurity attack?
- On whom is the duty imposed to prevent cybersecurity attacks?
- Does the severity and immediacy affect the response to cybersecurity attacks?
- Should cybersecurity be a national security matter?

Figure 2.6 Review questions.

3 Geopolitics and cybersecurity

INTRODUCTION

With respect to the relationship among nation-states, responding to a cyber attack is of particular, and growing, significance. One of the most important points of analysis regarding geopolitics is the possible response either to a cyber or countercyber attack, and how a particular measure will be perceived. Rearticulated: What kind of a response can be expected in the face of a cyber threat or during an actual attack? Given the range of responses stated earlier, national decision makers must assess how nation-states will react; for that reason, geopolitics highlights the importance of understanding both actual responses and reactions to those responses.

The following examples of cyber-related attacks and activities highlight the critical relationship between cybersecurity and geopolitics:

Example 1: Some suspect the Russian government of attacking or encouraging organized crime assaults on official websites in the nation of Georgia during military struggles in 2008 that resulted in a Russian invasion of Georgia.

Example 2: In 2009–2010, suspicions arose that a sophisticated government-created computer worm called **Stuxnet** was loosed in order to disable Iranian nuclear plant centrifuges that could be used for making weapons-grade enriched uranium. Unnamed sources and speculators argued that the governments of the United States and Israel might have designed and spread the worm.

Example 3: The American Defense Department has created a cyber command structure that builds Internet-enabled defensive and offensive cyber strategies as an integral part of war planning and war making.

Example 4: In May 2014, five Chinese military officials were indicted in Western Pennsylvania for computer hacking, espionage, and other offenses that were aimed at six U.S. victims, including nuclear power plants, metals, and solar product industries. The indictment comes after several years of revelations that Chinese military and other agents have broken into computers at major U.S. corporations and media companies in a bid to steal trade secrets and learn what stories journalists were working on.

Example 5: In October 2014, Russian hackers were purportedly discovered to be exploiting a flaw in Microsoft Windows to spy on NATO, the Ukrainian government, and Western businesses.

Example 6: The respected Ponemon Institute reported in September 2014 that 43% of firms in the United States had experienced a data breach in the past year. Retail breaches, in particular, had grown in size in virulence in the previous year. One of the most chilling breaches was discovered in July 2014 at JP Morgan Chase & Co., where information from 76 million households and 7 million small businesses was compromised. Obama administration officials have wondered if the breach was in retaliation by the Putin regime in Russia over events that occurred in Ukraine.

Example 7: Among the types of exploits of individuals in evidence today are stolen national ID numbers, pilfered passwords and payment information, erased online identities, and espionage tools that record all online conversations and keystrokes, and even hacks of driverless cars.

Example 8: Days before this report was published, Apple's iCloud cloud-based data storage system was the target of a so-called *man-in-the-middle* attack in China that was aimed at stealing users' passwords and spying on their account activities. Some activists and security experts said they suspected that the Chinese government had mounted the attack, perhaps because the iPhone 6 had just become available in the country. Others thought the attack was not sophisticated enough to have been government-initiated.*

---

* http://www.pewinternet.org/2014/10/29/cyber-attacks-likely-to-increase/, last viewed June 21, 2015.

Geopolitics refers to relations among nation-states and their engagement with the larger global community with particular emphasis on the relationship between geography and nation-state politics:

"Geopolitics takes as its task the disruption of geopolitical discourses: to study not the geography of politics within pregiven or commonsense places, but rather to foreground the politics of the geographical specification of politics. Security and geopolitics function in a dualistic manner. On the one hand, diplomacy and foreign policy are commonly conceived as highbrow issues shrouded in secrecy. On the other hand, and in parallel with this reliance on specialized language, discourse of security and geopolitics draw heavily on commonsense narratives about places and identities. Most geopolitical reasoning is not formal but practical. It draws on common sense rather than esoteric academic and technical arguments."*

In this chapter, the relationship between cybersecurity and *geopolitics* will be examined by analyzing particular examples reflecting the complexity of their confluence. The analysis will touch upon international law, specifically self-defense and proportionality. Nation-state decision making, reflecting predictability and consistency, significantly enhances global order. However, threats—whether actual or perceived—dramatically impact regional and global stability. In this vein, assessing how nation-states respond, whether unilaterally, bilaterally, or multilaterally, to particular crisis points is essential to understanding the practical impact of geopolitical considerations.

Effective geopolitics requires a confluence between the theoretical and the practical. The former demands that national leaders should understand a wide range of issues, including international law, international relations, finance, geography, and military power, particularly, its limits. The latter requires the implementation of these distinct disciplines with sensitivity, both to domestic politics and the global community, while recognizing the importance of tactical and strategic issues alike. Though, *prima facie*, tactical, and strategic considerations suggest a dissonance, effective national leaders are able to incorporate both in the decision-making process.

---

* See Kuus, M. *Geopolitics Reframed: Security and Identity in Europe's Eastern Enlargement*. Palgrave MacMillan, 2007 as cited in Amos N. Guiora, *Geopolitics*.

VIGNETTE

As mentioned earlier, geopolitics is the relations among nation-states and their engagement with the larger global community, with a particular emphasis on the relationship between geography and nation-state politics. The emphasis on geography and the larger global community plays a critical role in geopolitics.

Consider the following: It is in the year 1924, a horrific earthquake had hit Asia, affecting hundreds of thousands and potentially causing a tsunami thousands of miles away. However, due to the lack of information systems, there is not an adequate way to either warn those in the tsunami path, nor alert those to ask for assistance for the individuals hit by the earthquake.

Now, consider the year 2020. Not only is it quick to inform others in the path of the tsunami, it is even quicker to ask others for assistance for those affected by the earthquake. However, asking that may not always come with a result. We live in a world where news is processed 24/7, and there is constant information at our fingertips. On account of this, there is constant awareness of the endless atrocities and injustices that occur daily throughout different parts of the world. On any given day, there is a refugee crisis, a medical virus, a physical catastrophe, or a human-induced attack. It is often difficult to keep up with all these.

Thus, with geopolitics being the relations among nation-states and their engagement with the larger community, which are greatly affected by the increasingly globalized world in which we live. Consider the effect of an increasingly globalized world in the sense of cybersecurity.

As seen in Example 2, a virus, *Stuxnet* was loosed in order to disable Iran's nuclear capabilities. The implementation of this virus was widely reported on news channels and something that individuals throughout the world acknowledged. Not only this, the ability for whomever to introduce a virus into a country's nuclear capability is only possible due to the ever innovative techniques adapted by cyber.

In Iran, it is likely that other countries were made aware of nuclear capabilities either by their own reporting, or more likely by

(Continued)

surveillance information that recorded documentation of nuclear facilities either being built or currently existing. This technology came in the form of drones or other satellite surveillance. Thus, being an ever increasing globalized world, countries experienced concern knowing that a country, such as Iran, possessed these capabilities.

As seen with the earlier example, what if this had occurred in 1924? What if there was no way to even learn of these nuclear capabilities? Would it still be as great of a threat? Would we respond to it any differently? Would we prepare for the threat any differently? The confluence of technology has not only allowed us to create greater threats, it allows us to monitor greater threats.

In addition, if the introduction of information regarding a nuclear facility occurred in 1924, would there even be a possibility to destroy or severely impair the nuclear facilities, as the *Stuxnet* virus so aptly accomplished. Thus, not only has the introduction of information greatly shifted our perception on geopolitics, but how we can react to that information plays an even greater role.

Tactical thinking reflects decision making, focused solely on the *immediate*, whereas strategic thinking reflects a keen understanding of, and appreciation for, the *long term*, devoid of immediate results and impact. Perhaps, circumstances justify, or dictate, a narrow perspective. A global community implies enhanced cooperation across a wide range of issues, including finance, security, border control, environment, health care, and natural resources. National leaders, understandably, primarily emphasize domestic considerations; nevertheless, effective geopolitics suggests national interests are significantly enhanced when international affairs are *factored* into domestic decision making. In conjunction, a thorough geopolitics analysis includes the relationship between nation-states and corporations, and whether a duty exists for the protection of corporation within a nation-state. In addition, specific nation-states in particular and the international community, in general, are confronted with dilemmas regarding the limits of sovereignty in the face of actual or perceived threats.

For example: Challenges posed by Iran's commitment to development of a nuclear program have forced the international community to weigh distinct options regarding the limits of Iranian sovereignty and international intervention alike. The majority of the international community recognizes the threats a nuclear Iran poses, regionally and internationally alike. Nevertheless, concerns regarding fall-out from an armed attack on Iran have significantly contributed to imposition of wide-ranging economic and diplomatic sanctions, the effectiveness of which is an *open question.*

In determining the appropriate response to the threat posed by a nuclear Iran, the international community has demonstrated extraordinary discomfort regarding military measures. Although understandable, the broader question is, what are the ramifications, should the international community *not* prevent Iran from fulfilling its nuclear program? How national leaders engage in, and resolve, the decision-making process is essential to understanding the practical implementation of geopolitics.

SONY AND NORTH KOREA

For example, in considering the cyber attack on Sony, evidently undertaken by North Korea, three different countries are stakeholders (Figure 3.1).

Does that mean that two Japan and the United States were attacked? Answering that question requires addressing whether a cyber attack is akin to a traditional act of war. In traditional war, state A attacks physical targets in State B with tanks and planes, whereas a cyber attack is primarily an attack on private or public infrastructure. The attack's consequences may extend well beyond a physical attack: the impact of possibly shutting down a network or system goes beyond harm to a particular building, even if individuals are killed. Thus, the vulnerability of corporations, and their relation to the nation-state, recognizes a heightened sense of obligation to nation-states for their corporations. This expands the definition of geopolitics in a way separate from traditional terrorism. To that end, the consequences of a cyber attack can exceed those

---

- North Korea, purportedly responsible for the attack
- Japan, where Sony's corporate headquarters is located
- United States, where Sony Pictures Entertainment is located

---

Figure 3.1 Stakeholder country.

of a physical attack; attacking **critical infrastructure** goes beyond a **traditional attack** resulting in property damage or loss of life.

The significant impact of a cyber attack and the vulnerability it exposes justifies rearticulating core principles including threats, self-defense, and the scope and limits of responses. One of the most important questions in the context of geopolitics is whether a cyber attack justifies a physical response; if rearticulated, **can a nation-state physically attack a hacker**—state or individual—responsible for a cyber attack?

In considering the **confluence of geopolitics, cybersecurity, and self-defense**, a cyber attack poses a threat to individuals, corporations, and the nation-state. Although this legitimizes self-defense, the question necessarily is one of proportionality. According to Article 51 of the UN Charter, the nation-state has the right to engage in self-defense once attacked:

> "Nothing in the present Charter shall impair the inherent right of an individual or collective self-defense, if an armed attack occurs against a Member of the United Nations, until the Security Council has taken measures necessary to maintain international peace and security. Measures taken by members in the exercise of this right of self-defense shall be immediately reported to the Security Council and shall not in any way affect the authority and responsibility of the Security Council under the present Charter to take at any time such action as it deems necessary in order to maintain or restore international peace and security."*

When the United Nations was created, in the aftermath of World War II, nation-states were, largely, not in conflict with nonstate actors and terrorist organizations. However, in the subsequent decades, conflict has morphed from nation-states, confronting nation-states to nation-states confronting nonstate actors. Accordingly, a critical point of inquiry in the aftermath of a successful cyber attack is determining whether the responsible party is a nation-state or nonstate actor, either acting on its own behalf or that of a nation-state.

There are four different options that dictate how and when the state reacts to a cyber attack (Figure 3.2).

---

* http://www.un.org/en/documents/charter/chapter7.shtml, last viewed June 7, 2015.

- *Option #1*: a nonstate actor acting on its own behalf: if the attacker poses an immediate or future threat then the nation-state may define that individual as a legitimate target. Determination of future threat requires sufficient intelligence that justifies the nation-state's decision to "engage" that individual.
- *Option #2*: nonstate actor acting as a proxy (conduit) on behalf of a nation-state: the attacked nation-state is going to have to determine whether the legitimate target is the nonstate actor and/or the nation-state on whose behalf the nonstate actor conducted the attack.
- *Option #3*: a nation-state engaged in a cyber attack: if a nation-state engaged is engaged in a cyber attack it may be treated as an act of war and a responding nation-state must act according to the UN Guidelines.
- *Option #4*: nation-state acting as a proxy (conduit) on behalf of another nation-state.

Figure 3.2 State options.

VIGNETTE

With the above options listed out, it is helpful to apply each option to a real-life setting to further our understanding of how the options play out. *Option 1* focuses on a nonstate actor acting on its own behalf. This would occur when a corporation, say Sony, executed a cyber attack against another country. This is a role reversal from the situation we discussed later in the North Korea or Sony debacle. However, it is an important consideration to ponder. If Sony executed a cyber attack against North Korea, do they count as a legitimate threat, thus allowing North Korea to engage in self-defense pursuant to the UN Charter? North Korea must have sufficient intelligence that justifies their decision to engage Sony, but if they have such intelligence, the act of self-defense would be appropriate.

Option 2 focuses on a nonstate actor acting as a proxy (conduit) on behalf of a nation-state. Thus, consider, for instance, if Apple, acting under the direction of the U.S. government, hacked into thousands of user's phones in China. Can China

(Continued)

retaliate against the United States, pursuant to the UN Charter arguing self-defense? China would have to determine whether the target is justified on Apple or the U.S. government. This requires sufficient intelligence, as required in Option 1, and additional untangling to determine who the appropriate, legitimate target is.

Option 3 focuses on an actual nation-state engaged in a cyber attack. This scenario seems easiest in determining whether an attacked state can engage another nation-state under the guise of self-defense. If an actual nation-state is engaging in a cyber attack, it is most likely that it may be treated as an act of war, and the attacked state can act according to the UN Guidelines.

The final option, *Option 4* discusses the paradigm if a nation-state is acting as a proxy, or conduit for another nation-state. Take for instance, say the United States executed a cyber attack against Russia, acting for Ukraine. Would Russia have the ability, in self-defense, to execute a return cyber attack against United States? Or, pursuant to the UN Charter, would it be necessary to execute a return attack against Ukraine, because the United States was acting for Ukraine. This poses a more difficult question and, like all the options, requires sufficient intelligence before engaging in any form of self-defense.

WHO IS A LEGITIMATE TARGET?

For example—albeit not in the realm of cybersecurity: A number of years ago a terrorist attack in Israel resulted in the loss of innocent lives; it was determined that the organization responsible for the attack was based in Syria. Although the Israeli Air Force (IAF) attacked the terrorist organizations' training bases in Syria, Israeli officials claimed neither Syria nor Syrian sovereignty was the intended target. An important point of inquiry is whether the terrorist organization was acting on its own accord or as a conduit for Syria or Iran.

The decision to attack the training base suggests the larger question regarding the possible role of Syria or Iran was sidestepped. Nevertheless, sophisticated geopolitical analysis requires determining the relationship between the nation-state and nonstate actor in order to most accurately assess the identity of the legitimate target for a counterattack.

This argument would appear disingenuous at best as Syrian sovereignty was clearly violated by the breach of Syrian airspace by the IAF.

In contrast, the IAF attack on a facility identified as instrumental to Syrian efforts to develop nuclear capability is arguably different for the former raid was directed at terrorist bases (located in Syria), whereas the latter attack was aimed at specific Syrian targets. Nevertheless, both attacks violated Syrian sovereignty; the question is whether terrorism or counterterrorism justifies violating nation-state sovereignty when the nation-state is not the intended target.

North Korea's reported attack on Sony: If a nonstate actor (Group X) committed the attack on North Korea's behalf, the United States would have to resolve the following dilemmas in determining who is responsible for the attack: (1) Is Group X responsible for the attack, and (2) if the intelligence community can identify those actors, or are they legitimate targets, or is North Korea the legitimate target?

If the United States were to view North Korea as responsible for the attack on Sony, the decision whether to attack North Korea requires determining an attack on Sony Pictures is akin to attacking the United States. However, geopolitical and military realities unequivocally suggest attacking Group X is distinct from targeting North Korea. Although Sony is, doubtlessly, a substantial and important corporation attacking its intellectual property, it is not equivalent to committing an act of physical terrorism against American civilian targets. To note, a reader reading a previous draft disagrees with the suggestion and argues that an attack on a corporation is equivalent to an attack on the nation-state, being that corporations are essential to nation-states. The differences between cyber terrorism, conventional terrorism, and traditional warfare are highlighted by the questions given later.

VIGNETTE

As seen from the earlier examples, both with conventional terrorism and the North Korea or Sony example, determining a legitimate target is often the most disputed issue. However, it is not only the most disputed, it is the most critical. In order to respond, and to respond proportionally, that response must be directed against a legitimate target. Let us consider the following examples to continue our discussion of what constitutes a legitimate target.

(Continued)

Consider the following: you travel often for work; this week you are sitting in Washington Dulles Airport and you are accessing the airport's free Wi-Fi. This is a perk that many airports have implemented over the past few years, and one that many travelers not only access frequently, but they greatly benefit from it. Many travelers use this time to catch up on work, respond to correspondence, or catch up on the latest episode of their favorite show on Netflix.

However, many experts argue that the free Wi-Fi zones are hot pockets for cyber hackers. They say, by accessing the free Wi-Fi, you are simultaneously opening the front door and allowing cyber attackers to penetrate your computer system. Now, further imagine that a cyber attacker, accessing your information through a free Wi-Fi service at Washington Dulles Airport, is accessing it through their work computer at their office of employment.

This individual is not acting within the scope of his employment; however, he is using a work-issued laptop, work software, and is in a physical location that belongs to the corporation. Is the company a legitimate target? In response to the cyber attack, can the individual being attacked, the victim in this case, respond proportionally to the corporation? If not, why not? Is not the hacker using a work-issued computer, work software, and occupying a work-owned environment?

A legitimate target is difficult to define, not only for the earlier example but also in the inability to even define a cyber attacker. Consider the following. Imagine you are a victim of identity theft. As seen in later examples in the book, this is a problem all too common in the United States, as individuals steal another's social security number, and use that information to open credit cards, bank accounts, take out loans, and fully use their identity as their own.

The difficulty once this occurs is in the reparation. What tools are accessible to determine the cyber attack, who initially stole the identity? Once determined, can the individual respond proportionally against that individual? Are they a legitimate target? Not only that, imagine that your information is breached through a cybersecurity attack directed against Target, a popular departmental store. In the past few years, Target has been the victim of a cybersecurity breach, resulting in 70 million individuals losing their credit card privacy to hackers.

(Continued)

As a result of that, your identity has been stolen. Thus, different from the above example, you can now ascertain the company responsible for your identity being stolen; however, the actual individual doing the hacking is still unidentified. As the company has been identified, are they a legitimate target? Have they breached some duty, which results in them being responsible for the hack? Would it be proportional and legitimate for the victim to respond against them? Likely, at this point, no.

RESPONSES

The overarching question is whether a physical response is proportional in response to a cyber attack, or is the more appropriate response to a cyber attack a cyber counterattack? Rearticulated: Does a cyber attack on State A by State B warrant *only* a cyber counterattack or is physical engagement a legitimate and proportional response? (Figure 3.3).

The American response to the attack on Sony was a cyber counter attack; according to reliable sources the attack twice impacted North Korea's Internet infrastructure for at least two days. That, then, suggests the response to a cyber attack will be a **cyber counter attack**, rather than an attack **physically targeting** the person responsible for the initial attack. This model, distinct from the traditional operational counterterrorism response, has significant geopolitical ramifications for it illuminates the differences between cyber self-defense and traditional self-defense.

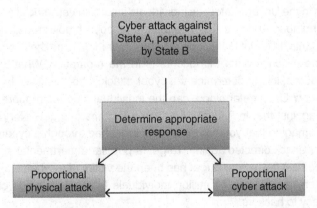

Figure 3.3 Response options.

Rather than targeting the individual responsible for the terrorist attack, cyber counterterrorism focuses on infrastructure, either of the attacking organization or the state. In the context of geopolitics and international law, the questions are twofold: (1) whether the state has been attacked and (2) what are the limits of a lawful response?

If the target is a corporation, then attacking a nation-state's Internet infrastructure is disproportionate; such a counterattack has the capability of significantly impacting hospitals, water systems, and modes of transportation. In the context of geopolitics, such a counterattack dangerously *ups the ante*. In the context of international law, it suggests a disproportionate response. Nevertheless, the nation-state has the right and obligation to respond: the question is **what are the tolerable limits of a response to a cyber attack**. The contours of geopolitics and international law suggest that strategic and legal restraints are inherent to the decision-making process.

VIGNETTE

There are three possible responses reflecting the sensitivity of broader, geopolitical considerations: (1) attacking North Korean targets directly that causes significant infrastructure damage, (2) a limited attack best defined as *message sending* with limited infrastructure damage, or (3) attacking a North Korean subsidiary or conduit rather than North Korea directly.

Let us consider the first option: attacking North Korean targets directly, causing significant infrastructure damage. In this scenario, America would launch a cyber attack against the core infrastructure of North Korea. This could involve the electricity grid, water system, traffic controls (for planes or cars), and a number of other options that would greatly affect the day-to-day life of North Korean residents. In doing so, the impact would be significant, more so than a limited physical counterattack that targeted specific individuals. Is that appropriate?

When considering the option of attacking North Korean infrastructure, one thing to consider is the effect the attack could have. A cyber attack on infrastructure has the ability to halt life, as it exists today. Is that appropriate in a circumstance similar to that

(*Continued*)

of the dispute between Sony and North Korea? Who is to decide whether it is appropriate? And finally, is there a barometer off which to measure the appropriateness of a countercyber attack?

The second option involves a limited attack against North Korea, more along the lines of *message sending*. This option triggers several questions—what constitutes a sufficient message? Does the message vary depending on the severity of the initial action? How can it be ensured the message was strongly received? Does affecting an electricity grid in one area of the country send an efficient message? How can a country determine which area to target when sending such a message? This option opens a Pandora's box of options that is difficult to control or measure the effectiveness or necessity of one over the other.

The third option diverts from a countercyber attack against North Korea and focuses on a countercyber attack against subsidiary or conduit of North Korea. In this scenario, the United States has been acting on behalf of Sony. Overall, North Korea did not come after the United States, rather they came after Sony. Thus, the United States acting in response to such an action is done so on behalf of Sony. Therefore, the third option involves the United States going after a similar subsidiary or conduit, like the Sony of North Korea. This poses similar questions from the second option. What conduit is appropriate to act on for the North Koreans? What level of correlation must exist between North Korea and the conduit to be a sufficient link for action? Overall, this option also creates an array of options that is difficult to regulate.

STUXNET

According to reliable sources, Iran's nuclear facility was attacked by a very sophisticated computer virus named Stuxnet.[*]

Most experts suggest that the virus was introduced either by Israel and/or the United States.

---

[*] http://www.wired.com/2014/11/countdown-to-zero-day-stuxnet/, last viewed June 21, 2015.

> • Did Israel and the United States violate Iranian sovereignty?
> • Did Israel and the United States engage in legitimate self-defense?
> • Did Israel and United States declare an act of war on Iran?

Figure 3.4 Geopolitical questions.

The relevant geopolitical and international law questions are listed in Figure 3.4. Answering these questions requires ascertaining whether Iran's nascent nuclear industry poses a threat to America and/or Israel and/or the broader world. As these lines are written, complex negotiations are being conducted regarding Iran's nuclear capability. The negotiations, regardless of their outcome, do not address broader international law and geopolitics questions regarding operational responses to the threat Iran poses, whether perceived, or actual. Over the past years Iranian leaders repeatedly threatened to attack Israel with nuclear weapons.

Prime Minister Netanyahu's clearly articulated warning that Israel would not hesitate to act preemptively convinced world leaders and that negotiating limits of Iran's nuclear capability was essential. From the perspective of international law, the rationale for Netanyahu's warning was Israel's right to self-defense. Although Netanyahu relied on Article 51, the basis for the negotiations reflects concern that threats and warnings would come to actual fruition, thereby significantly impacting the immediate region and larger international community.

Effective geopolitics suggests the importance of containing the threat in the context of crisis management and damage control. However, although regional stability is of extraordinary importance, the primary obligation of national leadership is the security and welfare of its civilian population. There is, then, a natural tension between national security as defined and implemented by specific nations and broader regional and international interests that extend beyond a particular nation-state.* Cyber significantly illuminates this tension:

"While the issue of cybersecurity has become one of great importance in U.S.–China relations, steps to address it remain

---

* https://www.fireeye.com/resources/pdfs/fireeye-wwc-report.pdf, last viewed June 21, 2015.

rudimentary in nature. On April 13, 2013, U.S. Secretary of State John Kerry announced that the two sides had agreed to establish a cybersecurity working group. A little over a week later, the chairman of the U.S. Joint Chiefs of Staff, General Martin Dempsey, convened a joint conference with Chinese General Fang Fenghui, who pledged to work with the United States because the consequences of a major cyber attack 'may be as serious as a nuclear bomb.' General Fang, the chief of the People's Liberation Army General Staff and a member of the Central Military Commission, indicated that he would be willing to establish a cybersecurity 'mechanism,' with the caveat that progress might not be swift."*

Conversations with leading experts shed light on the sophistication and complexity of Stuxnet. However, the technical aspects of the computer virus are beyond our purview; what is of interest is the nature of cyber conflict. In this vein, while Stuxnet's impressive technology has justifiably drawn significant attention, the broader inquiry focuses on its justifications and ramifications. In this vein, the decision taken by the Israel Defense Forces (IDF) Chief-of-Staff, Lt. General Gadi Eizenkot, to establish a Cyber Branch† reflects the threats and dangers posed by cyber warfare and terrorism. The branch will combine defensive and offensive capabilities reflecting the dramatically enhanced strategic significance of cyber warfare-terrorism security.

The combination of *offensive-defensive* capabilities, in the context of the international law principle of proportionality, suggest that attacking a nation-state's computer system is a legitimate form of self-defense, if the target poses a viable threat. The caveat: *The impact of a computer virus and other additional measures is contained to the target posing the perceived threat.* Regarding Iran, introducing a computer virus reflects proportionality if the self-defense measure is contained to a nuclear industry that can be used for offensive and aggressive purposes.

"Putting cyber attack in the context of military decision making (and assuming that state and nonstate actors overall have similar military planning processes) has implications for use of cyber

---

* http://www.carnegiecouncil.org/publications/articles_papers_reports/0156, last viewed June 21, 2015.
† http://www.ynetnews.com/articles/0,7340,L-4668912,00.html, last viewed June 20, 2015.

attacks. Nations are no more likely to launch a cyber attack that causes physical damage against the U.S. or its allies after Stuxnet than they were before its discovery, nor are they likely to stop using cyber techniques for espionage and political coercion. We have not seen physically damaging attacks that could cause damage, destruction, or casualties (as opposed to espionage and crime) against the U.S. and its allies from those countries with this capability because they assess the risk of a violent response as too high. This is the same reasoning that keeps them from launching aircraft or missiles against the U.S. However, international practice and law do not justify the use of force in response to espionage and crime, making the risk of a violent response small and acceptable.

To the credit of the designers of Stuxnet, it was carefully written to avoid collateral damage. Other attackers may not be so careful, but this has nothing to do with access to the Stuxnet code. Potential opponents still go through the same calculus of benefit and risk in deciding whether to use force against the U.S., and they are deterred by the likely U.S. military response using all military assets at its disposal, not just cyber attack. They may now cite Stuxnet as part of any public justification of attack, but this will be an excuse, not part of their decision making. Nations are no more likely to launch a cyber-attack against the U.S. or its allies after Stuxnet than they were before its discovery."[*]

Although the extent of the U.S. involvement in Stuxnet is unclear, a broad articulation of U.S. national security suggests significant American interests would be impacted were Iran to become a nuclear power. More directly—and perhaps acutely—Israeli national leaders have consistently argued that a nuclear Iran poses an existential threat to Israeli security. Although an open question, subject to intensive debate and diverse opinions, the introduction of Stuxnet clearly demonstrates the operational consequences of the relationship between cyber, geopolitics, and self-defense.[†]

---

[*] http://i-hls.com/2013/04/in-defense-of-stuxnet/, last viewed June 21, 2015.

[†] Simultaneous to the introduction of Stuxnet into Iran's developing nuclear industry, it is also been neither confirmed nor denied that a number of Iranian scientists, or those working with Iran on developing the nuclear industry, were killed in what would be called, for lack of a better term, a targeted killing. Those measures reflected aggressive self-defense in an effort to convince the Iranians to cease and desist developing their nuclear assets.

VIGNETTE

The caveat mentioned above is critical: **The impact of a computer virus and other additional measures is contained to the target posing the perceived threat.** However, can the impact of a computer virus be contained in such a way that it only addresses the target posing the perceived threat? Does the ability to implement a computer virus decrease the ability to contain said computer virus?

In addition, the caveat emphasizes the *perceived threat*. The additional question then becomes, how can one determine a perceived threat? There are many things that exist that could be perceived as a threat, but if countries reacted to every possible thing that could be perceived as a threat, they would run out of time and money. Therefore, the question then becomes, what threat constitutes a perceived threat, and at what level does that perceived threat justify the impact of a computer virus?

In furtherance of that question, is it possible to ensure that the computer virus is actually contained to the threat posed by the perceived threat? In addition, the question arises, is it possible to access the technology and information required to access and execute a computer virus that can be contained to a perceived threat and can actually ameliorate the said perceived threat? We live in an ever adapting and evolving technological world, and staying on top of it requires diligence and money. Often, those capable of executing the necessary computer virus or technique narrow down to a few individuals.

Thus, we not only have the question of what is a perceived threat, can a virus affect that threat, can the same virus affect only that threat and not pose too significant of an impact, but can we access that virus, and can we do so safely and through the hands of a trusted individual?

MOVING FORWARD

Tactically and short term, there is broad consensus that Stuxnet was deemed effective because it impacted the development of Iran's nuclear program. But what exactly is effective and how long is effectiveness analyzed? Perhaps of greater importance, from a geopolitical perspective, it highlights the requirement that nations with identifiable mutual interests recognize the cyber attacks, and cyber terrorism pose a threat to both individual countries and the broader international community. The development of strategic alliances—similar to NATO established in the aftermath of World War II to protect Western European countries from the Soviet Union and Warsaw Pact countries—in the face of cyber warfare or terrorism suggests efforts to protect nation-states from intangible, as compared to tangible, attacks.

Not only would such alliances be relevant to attacks coming from other countries, but also with respect to cyber attacks undertaken by nonstate actors. For example: ISIS (IS) is able to recruit new membership in Europe through the Internet and, in addition, to use the Internet for purposes of cyber incitement. In the context of geopolitics, the relevant question is whether like-minded countries should uniformly act to prevent the consequences of cyber recruitment and cyber incitement by shutting down websites. Doing so requires a rearticulation of threats and an understanding of the risks posed by the Internet and the recognition that warfare terrorism is morphing from a traditional physical attack to an intangible attack.

In reality, nation-states are facing threats from two distinct sources: physical attacks and intangible attacks. This transition, in the context of international stability and geopolitics, imposes significant new challenges on national decision makers. The power of the Internet, with respect to cyber warfare or terrorism, requires an understanding of the complexity of geopolitics and the link between geopolitics and cybersecurity. This suggests, in the context of international alliances and geopolitics, that stopgap measures including Stuxnet are strategically insufficient. To that end, NATO like alliance needs to be rearticulated, reimplemented, and restated to reflect this new threat of cyber attacks.

The questions that are to be considered in reviewing Chapter 3 are given on the next page (Figure 3.5).

- Does cybersecurity pose a geopolitical threat?
- How do nation-states effectively protect themselves?
- Is cybersecurity a global threat?
- What are the geopolitical consequences of a counter measure such as Stuxnet?
- Does cybersecurity pose a threat to national sovereignty?
- Does a cyber attack on a corporation justify an armed response by a state similar to a response to traditional terrorism?
- Does the fact Sony represent substantial economic interests impact U.S. decision-making?
- Where does the nation-state draw the line regarding self-defense?
- What are the arguments justifying a U.S. military response directed at North Korea?
- What are possible North Korean responses and how does that impact U.S. decision-making?
- Given a U.S. decision to attack North Korea will inevitably result in UN engagement, are U.S. decision makers willing to disclose intelligence information that justified the military response?
- What would be the U.S. response in the court of international public opinion?
- How does a nation respond to constantly evolving cybersecurity attacks?
- Does Stuxnet, an attack on Iran's nuclear centrifuges allegedly by the United States and/or Israel, constitute an attack on a sovereign state?
- What rules should govern the relations between nation-states regarding cybersecurity?
- Do nation-states have an obligation to work together against cybersecurity threats that impact multiple nation-states?
- Is sovereignty impacted by an attack on a nation's cybersecurity system?

Figure 3.5 Review questions.

4 International law and cybersecurity background

An important question to ask is whether or not the law applies to cybersecurity, and if the law applies to cybersecurity, what are the relevant legal structures?

How the nation-state responds to a cyber attack reflects the essence of international law, predicated on the nation-state's right to defend itself—when attacked—in accordance with Article 51of the UN Charter. The Charter's language suggests that the nation-state's right to engage in self-defense is limited to responding to an attack, reflecting an intellectual and practical dissonance. However, a broader reading suggests that the right to self-defense is legitimate in the context of preemptive self-defense. That right, in accordance with an enhanced understanding of Article 51, is predicated on the availability of intelligence information indicating that an attack is imminent. Imminence in the context of operational counterterrorism is limited to a specific individual deemed to pose a direct and immediate threat to national security.

Regarding cybersecurity, the intended target is the nation-state's Internet infrastructure. In contrast to traditional counterterrorism, cyber attacks target the nation-state's infrastructure, rather than seeking to kill an individual or bomb a building. The intended target of a cyber attack is infrastructure—whether the nation-states or the individuals—rather than physical or bodily harm. Despite the focus on infrastructure, not physical or bodily harm, the psychological harm is debilitating. The consequences, needless to say, are no less harmful and dramatic. After all, targeting a municipality's water system has significant ramifications and consequences, even though the *physicality* of the attack is not equated to a suicide bombing. Perhaps that distinction—physicality of a suicide bombing as compared to the means of a cyber attack—suggests that self-defense applied to the former is inapplicable to the latter. However, in the context of potential harm to the nation state and the right to engage in self-defense, that distinction does not *hold water* for it is unnecessarily self-limiting.

Adoption of such a model suggests that the nation-state would not be fully engaged in its primary obligation of protecting its civilian population. As discussed later, the question is one of practical applications and interpretation of international law.

VIGNETTE

Consider the following: self-defense is proper pursuant to Article 51 of the UN Charter assuming an attack is imminent. The operative term to satisfy in concluding whether a preemptive strike is necessary is the determination of imminence. Analyzing a situation and determining whether or not the imminence requirement is met is difficult. This debate arises specifically in a targeted killing context. In order to justify a targeted killing, namely, a drone strike, imminence must be satisfied. Specifically, the individual must be deemed to pose a direct and immediate threat to national security.

Thus, the following is considered:

> Defining imminence is essential to articulating and implementing a targeted killing paradigm predicated on the rule of law. Needless to say, that is far easier said than done. The difficulty is both in practice and principle; the former because decision makers prefer wiggle room, the latter because the term is, by nature, elusive, problematic, and subject to wide interpretation.[*]

As seen with the earlier definition, determining imminence is oft difficult but necessary in evaluating the need for self-defense. Self-defense seems to be only warranted if a specific individual poses a direct and immediate threat to national security. It is easier for a drone to see an individual preparing a bomb or gathering supporters who are planning to threaten the national security of the country. It is drastically different for a monitoring system, drone, or other tool to see an individual preparing a cyber attack, or currently engaged in a cyber attack.

(Continued)

[*] Guiora (2008).

With the inability to see a specific individual who is ready to pose a direct and immediate threat, does that mean self-defense against a cyber attack is never justified? Imagine that a suicide bomber successfully executes his or her plan and kills himself or herself, and several others, in a busy marketplace near a city center. With surveillance, if military intelligence was aware of the plot, knew the individual executing the plot, and saw him or her walking to the city center with a bomb, few would argue that the military did not have the right to eliminate the threat at that point.

It is clear, at this point, that without a preemptive act of self-defense, there will be casualties. Thus, pursuant to Article 51 of the UN Charter, self-defense is not only appropriate but expected. Now let us consider a different example. Imagine that at the same city center there is a busy sidewalk café. Within that café, a lone individual is sitting at a table typing on his laptop. Throughout the café, several others are doing the same, typing on their laptop intensely. Is it easy to predict who, if any, of those are a threat? At this point, is there a way to eliminate any threat? Is there a need for a preemptive act of self-defense? Likely no.

Now, imagine at the same time that lone individual is sitting in the café intensely typing on his laptop, a virus is loosed into the city's water system, shutting down the filtration system that cleans and purifies the water. Because of this, contaminated water now runs through all the pipelines that connect the city, resulting in water that is too unsafe to eat, drink, or even use for washing.

Has that individual now crossed the threshold that he or she deemed to pose a direct and immediate threat to national security? Imagine he or she has the capability to loose the same virus on every water system in America. However, it is virtually impossible for us to narrow down which computer worker introduced the virus. Thus, is it justified to take precautionary steps, before we can even get to this point, to eliminate the threat of contaminating the water system?

Imagine there are only so many people in America with the expertise and capability to introduce such a virus into the water system. Is the U.S. government justified in monitoring those individuals? Is it justified in tracking their movements and actions on a computer? If not, what is the best way to preemptively strike against an imminent cyber attack?

RIGHT TO SELF-DEFENSE

To that end, both in the context of terrorism—traditional (suicide bombing) and nontraditional (cyber attack)—the nation-state's right to engage in self-defense is predicated on the following. If viable, time relevant, corroborated, and reliable intelligence information is received that an attack is imminent, then Article 51 of the UN Charter may be applied reflecting legitimate self-defense in accordance with acceptable standards and principles of international law. Practically speaking, application of Article 51 grants the nation-state the right to attack proactively in order to prevent a successful cybersecurity attack.

That analysis is very similar to the right of the nation-state to act preemptively against an attack as traditionally defined and a cyber attack must be understood as similar to a physical attack. In that context, both an armed attack and an unarmed attack must be considered—with respect to self-defense—as intellectually and practically similar, regardless of the means applied. The nation-state's legitimate right to preemption, accordingly, extend to both forms of attack (Figure 4.1).

The *morph* from violent to nonviolent attacks, in terms of legitimate self-defense, is the essence of cyber attacks. Both the traditional and nontraditional reflect an attack on the nation-state, and in both paradigms the nation-state has the right to act proactively. That right extends to a potential attack emanating both from a state actor and nonstate actor.

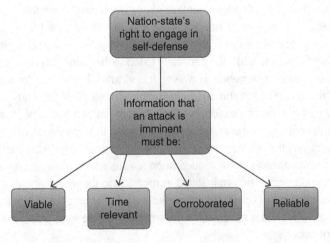

Figure 4.1 Nation-state's right.

In both instances—attack by state and nonstate actors alike—the nation-state has the right to preemptive self-defense. Both are predicated on a similar four-part analysis of intelligence information, in the context of a cyber attack, regardless of *point of origin*. Were available intelligence information to indicate a hacker is planning an attack intended to penetrate into the nation-state's computer infrastructure, thereby potentially causing significant harm, that individual is a legitimate target in the context of Article 51. From an operational perspective, the individual engaged in a potential cyber attack is a legitimate target in the same vein as an individual engaged in a potential physical attack, thereby expanding Article 51 to incorporate nonphysical armed attacks.

This expansive articulation of Article 51 incorporates both state and nonstate cyber actors, identified as responsible for a potential cyber attack, thereby defining both as legitimate targets. Therefore, a critical question in this discussion is whether a hacker is a legitimate target akin to an individual whose modus operandi is blowing up an office building, specifically and deliberately targeting the civilian population. The differences between the two actors are significant and must be acknowledged: a suicide bomber is manifestly intent on killing as many people as possible. Conversely, a cyber attacker is not focused on killing people, whereas deaths may be a *by-product* of the cyber attack.

VIGNETTE

Figure 4.1 demonstrates that a nation-state has the right to engage in self-defense if information about an imminent attack is viable, time relevant, corroborated, and reliable. Each factor plays a critical component in the imminence analysis. In addition, as mentioned earlier, imminence is the key in determining whether preemptive self-defense is a justified action. To fully understand what is required for a preemptive act of self-defense, and what is required to prove imminence, let us consider each factor individually.

The first factor involves viability. For something to be viable, it means something must be feasible, or capable of happening. For instance, if a perceived threat is imminent, decision makers must

(Continued)

analyze not only whether the threat is actually imminent, but more importantly whether the threat is viable. This specific analysis would turn on whether or not the threat could actually be carried out.

I would imagine that many decision makers, the president included, get numerous threats a day. Those receiving the threats then have the obligation to go through and determine whether or not the threat is capable of being carried out or viable. A similar analysis must go through a threat of an imminent cyber attack. Thus, a critical component of the imminence analysis is the viability of the threat, meaning the capability of it actually happening.

The second factor emphasizes relevance; specifically the threat is time relevant. This continues the viability point. For a threat to be imminent, it not only must be viable, but it must be time appropriate. Specifically, a threat that is set to occur 10 years down the road is likely not considered imminent compared to a threat that is set to occur tomorrow. In addition, a threat that has since passed its expiration date is not considered time relevant as well. The emphasis on time relevance plays hand-in-hand with the viability component. Meaning, not only must a threat be capable of being carried out, it must be carried out in an imminent fashion, meaning something that is soon to pass.

If a threat, either conventional or cyber, is set to be carried out in five years, there is good reason why the stress level regarding such threat would be lower. Most would argue there are more critical situations to discuss before that threat. In addition, many would argue that the situations and circumstances at that time will have likely changed, and there is a great possibility that the threat will not be carried out at that point. Ultimately, time relevance, like viability, is a critical component in the imminence analysis.

The third factor emphasizes whether the threat is corroborated. There are many methods to corroboration, and depending on how or when the threat is corroborated, it affects the ultimate analysis of imminence. Imagine a threat comes in from a source that is capable of carrying out the threat. Therefore, the threat is viable. In addition, that same threat is set to occur tomorrow. Therefore, the threat is time sensitive. However, the threat is full of unsubstantiated evidence and is unclear whether it will actually be executed.

(Continued)

A common way to corroborate a conventional terrorist threat is to monitor the chatter among the individuals involved. Often, surveillance teams can ascertain critical information through phone wires, e-mail chains, or social media accounts. This is a key form of corroboration. But, if a threat comes in that is viable and time sensitive, but is not corroborated, should it be justified as an imminent threat? Should the same justification analysis occur whether the threat is conventional terrorism or cyber?

Overall, the difficulty with corroboration is that it exists as almost a combination of both viability and time relevance. Because viability emphasizes ability or capability, corroboration plays in a similar field because corroboration relying on other sources emphasizes the capability or actuality of the threat. In addition, corroboration correlates with time relevance because corroboration from other sources often confirms the relevance or significance of the threat, and whether it is actually pertinent. Thus, corroboration is not only a critical, separate element, it also incorporates other components of the imminence analysis.

The final factor to consider is reliability. Reliability plays into viability, time relevance, and corroborated, but also exists as its own factor. Reliability of the threat, and the source presenting the threat, emphasizes the necessity to corroborate. In order to corroborate, the first step would be to determine the source's reliability. Thus, those two factors play hand in hand.

Imagine the following: a threat has been issued against a city in the United States. This threat comes from a known terrorist organization that has executed attacks in the past and has vowed to execute attacks in the future. The group has promised physical harm to a specific city by a specific date. Is the threat imminent? Does it satisfy viability, time relevance, corroborated, and reliable? Absolutely.

If the threat comes from a known terrorist organization, that suffices both corroborated and viability. The threat is corroborated because it is from an organization, previously designated as a terrorist organization, meaning they have either carried out past attacks or vowed to carry out attacks in the future. In addition, the threat is viable because the organization has previously demonstrated its capabilities and its destructive nature in the past.

(Continued)

The same threat suffices time relevant because it is an ongoing event. Because the group has executed attacks in the past, and vowed to in the future, it seems the threat of a similar attack is an ongoing threat that is certainly time relevant. In terms of reliability, the threat suffices the reliable prong because it is something that has been done in the past and can easily be recreated in the future. Thus, it is easy to say that the threat is imminent, and preemptive self-defense is warranted pursuant to Article 51 of the UN Charter.

Now, consider the same organization that has executed conventional terrorist attacks in the past and has vowed to breach a city's water system and has shut down the filtration system so as to contaminate the water supply. Does the threat fit the same requirements as the threat of conventional terrorism? Does it matter that the threat differs from its previous terrorist action? What analysis must be done to determine whether the threat is viable? How does one ascertain whether or not the terrorist organization is actually capable of accomplishing such a feat?

Ultimately, the imminence analysis is increasingly more difficult because many times, with cyber, it is a novel situation that has never been addressed previously. In addition, it is often difficult to measure whether or not an individual or organization actually has the capability to measure out such an attack. Overall, the imminence analysis involving viability, time relevance, corroboration, and reliability is still a critical component of the analysis, whether it is with conventional terrorism or cyber attack.

IMPACT OF CYBER ATTACK—VULNERABILITY OF INFRASTRUCTURE

A cyber attack has the potential of causing significant damage to the nation-state's infrastructure, ranging from the water system to air traffic control towers.

Although the movie *Die Hard 2** illustrates the dangers and consequences of a successful hacking into an airport's security system, the

* http://www.imdb.com/title/tt0099423/.

reality of this danger was self-evident when I was invited to observe the landing process of a commercial jetliner. Although the competence, professionalism, and extensive training of the pilots were readily apparent, similarly, apparent, however, was the extraordinary complexity of the multiple *moving pieces* required to both guarantee passenger safety and ensure the plane's safe landing. This can be rearticulated as follows: An interaction between the pilots and air traffic control stations in different countries, communicating with pilots of additional aircraft flying within *eye contact* distance of each other, highlighted the potential threat posed by a cyber attack.

This reality was clearly articulated in a conversation I had with a former head of the Israel Security Agency.*

When asked what is the one incident that *wakes you up at 3 a.m.*, his response was immediate and concise. Without any deliberation, my interlocutor responded: *an attack on EL-AL.†*

When I asked him to expound on his response, he answered: "Not only would the attack result in the loss of hundreds of lives, but it would demand an extraordinary operational response by the government."

Although I asked the question focusing on a physical attack, the query—and response—reflects an approach applicable to a nonphysical attack. In both instances—physical and cyber attack—the consequences would be similar: an extraordinary loss of life and a powerful response in the context of aggressive operational counterterrorism. However, often nation-states vary on their prioritization—on what demands the most resources—physical or cyber attack.

INTERNATIONAL LAW AND LEGITIMATE TARGET: WAR AND CYBERSECURITY ACCORDING TO INTERNATIONAL LAW

It is for that reason, then, that in considering the relationship between international law and cybersecurity, the conclusion that a cyber hacker may also be considered a legitimate target in the context of operational counterterrorism is warranted. However, caveats and limits are essential. With respect to traditional terrorism, defining an individual as a legitimate target has potential dramatic consequences in the context of a targeted killing or drone attack. Expanding drone attacks or targeted

---

* I interviewed (by telephone) the former head for a previous book project.
† The Israeli National Airline.

killing to include a cyber attacker reflects a significant broadening of the operational application of Article 51; this proposed expansion suggests, then, that a cyber attacker is considered akin to an individual engaged in a physical attack.

This expansion weighed carefully for the consequences, both in principle and operationally, is significant: An individual responsible for a nonphysical attack will be considered with the same gravity as an individual responsible for a physical attack directly resulting in the loss of lives. The importance cannot be sufficiently emphasized: the by-product of a cyber attack may be a loss of lives; the direct intention of a physical attack is the loss of lives and yet, in accordance with this proposed model, those responsible for both manners of attack would be considered legitimate targets of a drone attack or targeted killing.

The decision to define a specific hacker as a legitimate target for aggressive operational counterterrorism would depend on an assessment that no other means to neutralize the individual are possible. As is the case with a potential suicide bomber, the preference—and emphasis—is on detaining the individual. However, if that proves operationally nonfeasible and the cyber attack endangering national security is imminent, then preemptive self-defense justifies measures similar to those implemented against an individual planning a physical attack. This is the essence of a legitimate target, regardless of the nature of the planned attack (Figure 4.2).

The earlier discussion focused on the triangular relationship between the nation-state, the nonstate actor, and cybersecurity in the context of Article 51. In examining the limits of Article 51, we next consider whether a cyber attack undertaken by a nation-state, or a third party acting on behalf of the nation-state against another nation-state, justifies implementation of Article 51. This can be rearticulated as follows: Is a cyber attack by nation-state directed at another nation-state akin to a traditional act of war?

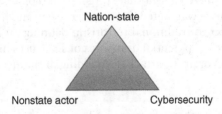

Nation-state

Nonstate actor   Cybersecurity

Figure 4.2 Nation-state triangle.

The ramifications and consequences are significant: Should the attacked nation-state conclude that a cyber attack by a nation-state (or conduit) is equivalent to an armed attack, then the logical inference is that a state of war may exist between the two nation-states. Should the nation-state conclude a cyber attack is akin to an act of war—and consequently declare war—then the significance of a cyber attack has been profoundly enhanced.

Two examples facilitate this discussion (Figure 4.3).

The consequences of this extended interpretation, and the subsequent application of Article 51 and the Laws of War, suggest a complex and complicated paradigm regarding the consequences of undertaking a cyber attack. In applying international law, the United States would be required—were it to conclude that a cyber attack is equivalent to an armed attack—to present a compelling argument that a cyber attack is, indeed, an attack justifying a counterattack.

The requisite follow-up question is whether the counterattack would be limited to a cyber counterattack, or would international law tolerate an armed attack in response to a cyber attack. Should the United States determine that the initial cyber attack constituted an act of war, then the decision to engage—to determine the means and method—would be in accordance with the accepted principles and practices of international war.

We return to the question of the manner in which the response to an act of war is conducted. Simply put: Is the legitimate response to a cyber attack by a nation-state a cyber counterattack or is traditional, armed attack lawful? The essential question is to determine the limits of legitimate self-defense. Although the answer depends on a multitude of circumstances, criteria, and harm caused, the broad parameters would perhaps suggest that the most appropriate response to a

---

- *Example 1*: If U.S. decision makers conclude that an attack on Sony is equivalent to an attack on the United States, then that cyber attack (whether directly by North Korea or indirectly by a third party conduit) justifies the United States' declaration of war against North Korea;
- *Example 2*: If U.S. decision makers conclude hacking into U.S. government computer infrastructure was conducted by Chinese hackers then, and that this hack was tantamount to an attack against the United States then, in principle, the United States could declare war against China.

Figure 4.3 Critical examples.

cyber attack is a cyber counterattack rather an armed attack. Criteria to consider vary from how the damage was caused and the amount of damage caused.

This *appropriateness* is viewed both through the lens of international law and the court of international law; it is doubtful that the international community would view favorably a military attack in response to a cyber attack. The opposition would largely focus on the international law principles of proportionality and military necessity. However, a limited military response—specifically targeting either state actors or nonstate actors acting as conduits for the nation-state— would conceivably be understood to reflect a measured state response in the context of limited self-defense. Nevertheless, the legitimacy and lawfulness of the state action would depend on successfully, and compellingly, demonstrating a link between the attacking state and the cyber attack.

With respect to the North Korea–United States paradigm, the legitimacy of the United States' response would be significantly enhanced were the response an Internet attack on North Korea rather than a traditional military attack on North Korea. This means that the tank versus tank paradigm applicable to traditional warfare would not be relevant to cybersecurity or cyber self-defense. Rather, the acceptable response would be limited to a cyber counterattack on that nation's infrastructure. Rather than attacking physical targets, the legitimate target (in the state–state paradigm) will be limited to the nation-state's computer system rather than a physical target. This proposal reflects a balancing approach that simultaneously recognizes the fact that a cyber attack is akin to an act of war while limiting self-defense to a cyber, rather than physical, counterattack. Implementation of this model requires that the attacked nation-state have available very sophisticated cyber countermeasures capable of penetrating the attacking nation-state's infrastructure.

THREE PARADIGMS: PRACTICAL APPLICATION OF INTERNATIONAL LAW

There are, then, three relevant paradigms with respect to the confluence between international law and cybersecurity (Figure 4.4).

The practical application of the three paradigms requires the nation-state to develop an operationally viable cyber counterattack policy and capability. Doing so ensures that the nation-state conducts self-defense in accordance with existing international law principles; this

---

1. The nation-state has the right to protect itself against both an attacking nation-state and nonstate actor responsible for a cyber attack;
2. Attacking a nation-state's infrastructure justifies a response; the operative question is whether the legitimate response is restricted to a cyber counter attack against the attacking state's Internet infrastructure or physical engagement targeting the state specifically identified as responsible for the cyber attack;
3. The conduit, acting on behalf of the nation-state, presents a dilemma distinct from the nonstate actor and more akin with the nation-state model; operational decision making regarding the conduit, in the context of self-defense, is dependent on a number of factors including whether the Internet infrastructure is a readily identifiable target, the degree of determinable involvement by specific individuals, and the damage caused to the nation-state.

Figure 4.4 Relevant paradigms.

is essential to a legitimate application of the principle of proportionality. The attacked nation-state, in order to meet the proportionality in the context of international law, must develop cyber countercapability in response to a cyber attack. The importance of cyber countercapability is that it simultaneously facilitates self-defense while respecting international law principles.

VIGNETTE

The first paradigm emphasizes the nation-state having the right to protect itself against both an attacking nation-state and a nonstate actor responsible for a cyber attack. First, let us assume, for assumption sake only, Russia launches a nuclear weapon against the United States. It seems very few people, if anyone, would argue that the United States now has the right to a proportional response in self-defense. Now, let us assume, Russia has launched a cyber attack against the United States; specifically, it has shut down all computer systems at air traffic control towers at every airport in America. Because of this, none of the flight technicians is able to direct the airplanes taking off, landing, or flying in the sky.

(Continued)

This is a significant risk. Without the air traffic control tower, planes do not know whether they can land successfully, if they are flying on the same flight path as another plane, or whether they are cleared for take off. This could result in a significant number of deaths. Thus, just as the nuclear weapon justifies a proportional response in self-defense, so does the shutting down of air traffic control towers. In terms of a counter cyber attack, a cyber attack by a nation-state against another nation-state is an easier question to answer in terms of proportional self-defense.

Now, let us assume for the sake of example, the air traffic control towers were shut down, but not by Russia. This time they were shut down by an independent agency operated in Russia, with Russian employees, but acting independently. Is the United States justified in a counter cyber attack against Russia? Is it justified in a counter cyber attack against the independent agency? Does it have to be one or the other, or is the United States justified in a cyber counterattack against either Russia, the independent agency, or both? These are the difficult questions to answer with cyber attacks.

With the second paradigm, the operative question is whether the legitimate response is restricted to a counter cyber attack against the attacking state's Internet infrastructure or physical engagement targeting the state responsible for the cyber attack. So, continuing with our previous example, imagine Russia has launched the cyber attack against the United States air traffic control towers. If a response is justified, which most would argue it is, can the United States response be a cyber attack only, or is it justified in self-defense in perpetuating a physical attack against Russian forces? Is a physical act of war a proportional response to a cyber attack?

Finally, with the third paradigm, we will continue with the earlier example. What if, after the attack on the air traffic control towers, it is determined that the independent agency was acting on behalf of Russia. Can the United States engage in a proportional counterattack against Russia? Or does it have to be against the independent agency? Further, can the United States engage in a physical attack, either against Russia, or the independent agency, or must it stick with a proportional counter cyber attack? These are all difficult questions that arise from cyber attacks.

MOVING FORWARD

If the United States were to make the argument that an attack on every American asset, corporation, or individual is akin to attacking America, the *self-defense door* opens beyond what international law should reasonably tolerate.

To that end, the following is recommended as reflecting a balanced approach: An attack on Sony—if defined as an attack on the United States—should be responded to only with a cyber counter attack. That response must be proportional, aimed exclusively at the attacking states' cyber infrastructure rather than at a physical target. A viable argument cannot be made that a specific individual—conduit or state actor—can be targeted in response to an attack on a corporation. However, if the individual involved in cyber attacking has the imminent potential to cause physical harm, then that person is a legitimate target subject to the caveats previously discussed.

In accordance with international law, the response to a cyber attack must be proportional, the intelligence information must indicate that an attack is imminent, and the nation-state must demonstrate there were no alternatives to physical engagement. If these criteria are met in their entirety, then the nation-state has the ability to physically engage someone who has the potential to cause physical harm to the nation's civilian population including a cyber attack. That does require recognition that international law, with respect to self-defense, need be rearticulated to account for cyber attack and its consequences.

The following are questions to consider while reviewing Chapter 4 (Figure 4.5).

- Does international law apply to cybersecurity?
- Does international law allow nation-states to protect themselves from cyber attacks?
- Is an attack on a corporation the same as an attack on a nation-state?
- How is a legitimate target defined in a cyber attack?
- Should a certain level of cooperation exist among government entities, local law enforcement, and corporate bodies?
- Do countries have an obligation to share relevant information regarding cyber security concerns or attacks with one another?

Figure 4.5 Review questions.

5 Development and implementation of cybersecurity policy

INTRODUCTION

In this chapter, the focus will be on the development and implementation of cybersecurity *policy*. Policy requires a thorough, interdisciplinary analysis of the issue in order to develop the most effective responses to the threat posed by cyber attacks.

In the context of examining the policy, the first question we have to ask ourselves is whether or not we can truly defend ourselves against cyber attackers. In the context of policy, if there is no effective countermeasure to cyber, then developing a cyber counterpolicy poses extraordinary challenges. Accordingly, a policy is dependent on effective practical measures responding to cyber attacks and cyber threats.

One of the critical questions in developing a cyber counterpolicy is determining the definition of *effective* cyber countermeasures. The importance of the relationship between policy and effectiveness of countermeasures cannot be sufficiently emphasized. In many ways, the two must be congruent, reflecting coherence and symmetry. This is particularly difficult when both the nature of cyber threats and the requisite counterthreats are best defined as comprised of multiple moving pieces. It is akin not only to a jigsaw puzzle but also a jigsaw puzzle that reflects more unknowns than known.

QUESTIONS TO ASK

The questions that demand our attention are complex; they also highlight the inherent uncertainty of cybersecurity, much less the articulation and implementation of a coherent policy. The first question considers whether or not all cyber attacks can be prevented. Although the answer is, clearly, no, it is important to recall that national decision makers are engaged in rhetoric which creates the illusion that *terrorism can be defeated*, thereby establishing both false expectations and unattainable goals. This is inherently dangerous as the public, in the aftermath of such pronouncements, can reasonably (from its perspective) assume that it is fully protected from terrorism and cyber attacks. This is, needless to say, a false paradigm with negative consequences from a policy and public perspective alike.

The second question considers whether cybersecurity is effective, if 50% or 75% of known attacks are neutralized. The third question determines whether the correct *measuring stick* regarding effectiveness is purely qualitative? If, for example, a large attack is prevented but a series of small attacks are successful (from the attackers' perspective), does that mean that cybersecurity policy is ineffective?

Fourth, does the prevention of one major attack reflect effective cybersecurity policy? In addition, are there some targets—the Pentagon as an example—that the successful prevention of a cyber attack is so important from a national security perspective that in order to ensure its prevention, other attacks are tolerable? Albeit difficult to determine which attacks qualify as tolerable and which do not, it begs the question as to what cost we are willing to bear to avoid attacks on critical infrastructure, such as the Pentagon.

The question is asked in the context of *resource prioritization, cost-benefit analysis, and risk assessment* (Figure 5.1).

Similarly, in the context of this proposed triangle, what is the impact significance of a *hack of individual credit cards*? To what extent, from a policy perspective, does this (hacking of individual credit cards) warrant significant attention and resources? And finally, from a policy perspective, what is the impact of a successful hack of a *major health or insurance corporation* resulting in the exposing of private records?

Answering these questions requires *national security officials, senior business executives, thought leaders, law enforcement officials,*

Figure 5.1 Resource triangle.

and politicians to articulate an implementable, practical, and legal cybersecurity/counter cybersecurity policy. This poses enormous challenges, because the essence of a policy predicated on the rule of law necessarily reflects recognition of the *limits of state power.*

VIGNETTE

In considering the questions above, walking through an example will help to demonstrate the difficulty that comes with each question. The first question considers whether or not all cyber attacks can be prevented. Imagine a large corporation, specifically one in the business of holding individual's personal records, like a hospital system. You are the chief executive officer (CEO) of this hospital system and your chief intelligence officer tells you it will cost an astronomical cost each year to build up protection against a potential cybersecurity attack.

In addition, there is no guarantee that the attack would even occur or that the protection would even be effective. If you are in the business of making your company profitable, as most CEOs are, are you likely to pay the astronomical amount for protection against a potential attack with the possibility that the protection is not even effective? Likely not.

The second question considers the effectiveness of a cybersecurity system. Is a cybersecurity protection system effective, if it neutralizes only 50%–75% of cyber attacks? Imagine you are the CEO of the company in the previous paragraph and the cost of cybersecurity protection is significantly greater than any loss suffered by 50% of cyber attacks. Meaning, as a company, you are paying more in protection, however, the threat of loss is not that significant. Would it be worth to continue to pay for cybersecurity protection? Likely not. Would it be prudent? Absolutely.

The third question considers an adequate *measuring stick* in determining the effectiveness of a cybersecurity policy. It seems that effectiveness would be measured by how many cyber attacks the policy thwarted, in order to determine whether a policy is effective. However, oftentimes it is difficult to determine how many attacks were thwarted, because they did not occur; therefore, there

(Continued)

is no data demonstrating the effectiveness of the policy. The difficulty in measuring the effectiveness further plays into the decision of the CEO in determining whether it is cost worthy to invest in such a protection mechanism.

The final question to consider is whether the prevention of one major cybersecurity attack reflects an effective cybersecurity policy. This plays more to the side of encouraging a CEO to invest in such a policy. By demonstrating to both the CEO as well as the shareholders that the policy saved them thousands of dollars, hours spent recovering lost data, and reputation points, the CEO and shareholders will be more likely to invest in the astronomical costs.

Each of these paradigm questions demonstrates the difficulties in creating a cybersecurity policy. These difficulties exist at each level and are often difficult to navigate and find common ground among directors.

CREATING POLICY

Creating effective, cyber policy rooted in the limits of power requires *narrowly* defining what assets demand protection. This demands stakeholders to thoroughly and realistically analyze vulnerability and capability. The analysis is significantly enhanced by implementation of the *triangulation model* explained in the previous section.

Policy cannot be viewed in a vacuum; there must be careful considerations to tactical and strategic considerations reflecting recognition of short-term and long-term goals. Regarding cybersecurity, policy is impacted by the scale of vulnerability manifested by the number of attacks and the failure by various stakeholders to fully articulate implementable countermeasures. An exchange with experts from different countries suggests a paradigm reflecting *trial by error*.

While understandable given the relative newness of the threat combined with demonstrated uncertainty regarding response mechanisms, the result is, largely, a policy that suggests a heavy weight boxer dazed in the ring. This is not to suggest that the stakeholders will not develop more effective policies and response models, but the consistent string of successful cyber attacks indicates that effective cyber prevention-response models require significant attention.

Overall, cyber cannot be prevented 100%, and there are significant psychological ramifications.

Defining terms is essential to policy development; it is to that discussion we direct our attention.

DEFINING TERMS—EFFECTIVENESS

This definition incorporates the following premises: (1) terrorism is not 100% preventable; (2) counterterrorism must have a short-term (tactical) as well as a long-term (strategic) component; and (3) counterterrorism must be conducted while balancing competing interests of human life, financial cost, and civil liberty.

Terrorism is not 100% preventable

Security analysts are wont to frame recommended counterterrorism measures in an effectiveness paradigm that demands foolproof safeguards. However, it must be clearly stated that terrorism is not 100% preventable. Simply because a terrorist attack succeeds does not mean existing counterterrorism measures are ineffective. The inverse is also true: The absence of terrorist attacks does not necessarily indicate existing counterterrorism measures are effective.

VIGNETTE

Consider this first point that in analyzing effectiveness, a critical concept to accept is that terrorism is not 100% preventable. In addition, as mentioned above, it is further difficult to measure the effectiveness of counterterrorism measures based on the existence or lack of a terrorist attack. Thus, the first prong of the effectiveness definition, that terrorism is not 100% preventable, is critical to accept before a solid cybersecurity policy can be created.

Thus, with the acceptance that terrorism is not 100% preventable, what is a benchmark to measure against? What is a percentage that we are happy with? More specifically, if the cybersecurity counterterrorism measures prevent against 50% of terrorist attacks, is that enough? Or is 75% enough? Or, is there even a set amount, or is it more based on the type of attacks that are prevented?

(Continued)

Ultimately, it is incredibly difficult to measure the effectiveness of a cybersecurity policy on numbers or set percentages.

The understanding that terrorism is not 100% preventable is necessary, because it furthers the policy's capabilities if there is an inherent understanding that things may go wrong. For example, say there was a cybersecurity attack that likely could have been prevented but was not. At that point, many lawmakers may argue it is not worth investing hundreds of thousands of dollars in a counterterrorism cybersecurity policy, because it does not work, is not effective, and is therefore, a waste of money. However, that is inaccurate. Thus, the acceptance that terrorism, both conventional and cyber, is not 100% preventable allows for flaws or missteps in the policy and its ability to move forward.

Counterterrorism must have a short-term as well as a long-term perspective.

If a counterterrorism strategy only targets short-term threats, it will likely overlook other (long-term) real threats. It is important to note that terrorist organizations define effectiveness through the prism of long-term strategic considerations. To understand the terrorist mindset, it is necessary to appreciate the determination, resilience, and single-mindedness with which terrorists work. Terrorists are willing to engage in a war of attrition with enormous personal hardship for the individual and his immediate family to achieve specific goals.

VIGNETTE

This understanding is critical. In furtherance of the effectiveness definition, the second prong emphasizes the short-term as well as the long-term perspective. Not only that, the second prong goes hand-in-hand with the first prong, in recognizing that terrorism is not 100% preventable. To better understand this second prong of the effectiveness definition, it is critical to review the definition of terrorism, as listed in earlier chapters.

We previously defined terrorism as an act, by an individual or a group, intended to kill innocent individuals, primarily as a way of

(Continued)

instilling fear in others, with the purpose of advancing one of the four causes—political, religious, social, and cultural—with respect to government policy. Thus, terrorism has no specific end date; rather, those vowing to the cause will continue as they advance one of the four causes, and will continue to do so until they feel they have been successful.

Thus, if a cybersecurity policy attempted to be effective, and only had a short-term mentality, it would not even scratch the surface of the potential counterterror measures that need to be incorporated. However, if a cybersecurity policy only focused on long-term goals, it is likely to miss critical points of penetration that exist in the short-term mindset. Thus, for a cybersecurity policy to really be effective, it must have a short-term as well as a long-term perspective.

Consider the following example: A known terrorist organization, one that is designated by the U.S. government as a terrorist organization, has taken control of an air traffic control tower in Detroit and is now directing planes, telling them where to land, what altitude to fly at, and when to take off. In addition, with enhanced voice technology, the planes being communicated with are unaware that the air traffic control tower has been compromised and are following all directions being given to them.

Now, for a short-term counterterrorism cybersecurity policy, it would focus solely on how to regain control or access of the air traffic control tower. The situation is imminent and requires immediate response in order to minimize the threat of lives. However, it is critical to also recognize that the same counterterrorism cybersecurity policy that focuses on the short term must also focus on the long term. If the policy only focuses on the short term and only solves this problem, the incident is likely to occur again.

Thus, it is critical that the policy understands the motivations of the terrorist organization, and in doing so, implements long-term and short-term counterterrorism cybersecurity goals to be truly effective.

Counterterrorism must be conducted while balancing competing interests of human life, financial cost, and civil liberty.

Finding a balance between national security and the rights of individuals is the most significant issue faced by liberal democratic nations developing a counterterrorism strategy. Without a balance between these two tensions, democratic societies lose the very ethos for which they fight. As Benjamin Franklin once said, "those who would give up essential liberty, to purchase a little temporary safety, deserve neither liberty nor safety." Indeed, it is imperative for democracies to avoid infringing on political freedoms and civil liberties. Yet, a government's ultimate responsibility is protecting its citizens. This struggle to balance competing interests may be the most fundamental dilemma confronting democracies today.

Counterterrorism, both strategically and tactically, must be premised on this reality. Engaging in a never-ending cycle of violence is one means by which terrorist organizations signal to various audiences (the general public, followers, and the relevant government) their commitment to the cause. From the geopolitical perspective of terrorists, pressure exerted by an attacked and affected public on the relevant government justifies continued attacks on innocent civilians.

The first step in creating an effective counterterrorism measure is analyzing the threat. To that end, the questions raised in Figure 5.2 must be answered.

Once these questions are answered, the threat can be placed on an imminent continuum with the understanding that one large threat may be comprised of smaller, more manageable, threats. The imminent continuum has four major benchmarks:

Imminent: Imminent threats are those that are to be shortly conducted; for example, a hot intelligence report suggests that a bomb will be detonated tomorrow at 9:11 a.m. at a domestic terminal at JFK airport.

Foreseeable: Foreseeable threats are those that will be carried out in the near future (with no specificity); therefore, they are more distant than an imminent threat, for example, a foreseeable threat would be premised on valid intelligence

---

- What is the threat the state faces?
- Who is responsible for planning the threat?
- Who is responsible for financing the threat?
- Who is responsible for carrying out the threat?
- When will the threat likely be carried out?

Figure 5.2 Counterterrorism questions.

indicating terrorists will shortly begin bringing explosives onto airplanes in liquid substances.

Long-range threats: Long-range threats are those that may reach fruition at an unknown time; for example, terrorists' training with no operational measure specifically planned would fit in this category.

Uncertain threats: Uncertain threats constitute those that invoke general fears of insecurity. As a result of train bombings in England and Spain, travelers in the United States might potentially or conceivably feel insecure riding trains without bolstered security. This would be true regardless of whether there is valid intelligence indicating terrorists intent to target trains in the United States.

VIGNETTE

In order for a cybersecurity counterterrorism measure to be effective, it must be recognized that 100% prevention is not practical, and to consider both the long term and the short term. However, the third and arguably most important prong of the effectiveness of cybersecurity policy emphasizes the balance between national security and the rights of individuals. As mentioned above, in receiving and comprehending a cybersecurity threat, the first thing that should be done is answering the following question. Let us walk through each question with a pertinent example.

Consider for a moment that it is a Tuesday morning in April; the White House has received an online video from a known intelligence organization that promotes harm to the United States. The message touts the shutdown of the electrical grid of the state of Texas in 24 hours, unless certain demands are met. The first step, as mentioned above, is walking through pertinent questions in measuring the threat.

The first question emphasizes the actual threat and considers what is the threat that the country faces. In this instance, the threat is a shutdown of an electrical grid. This is a significant threat. This threat is not significant, not just due to the size of the threat (making the whole state of Texas go black), but also due to the ramifications that come with shutting off an entire electrical grid. Without electricity,

(Continued)

metro rail systems cannot function, offices cannot work, and the descent of darkness often results in lawless and chaotic behavior. Thus, the threat is viable and real and seemingly imminent.

The second question in analyzing the threat discusses who is responsible for planning the threat. If this threat came from a no-name organization, rather than an individual living in a small town somewhere far away who likely does not have the ability to carry out the threat, the analysis will be rated lower. However, if this threat comes, like it did, from a designated terrorist organization with proven capabilities in the past, the threat will be given greater weight.

The third question involves finances and considers who is responsible for financing the threat. This furthers the analysis above, as financing from a lone individual is less likely to be effective as it is with financing from a designated terrorist organization. The fourth question, who is responsible for carrying out the threat, also furthers the above analysis. The lone individual's capabilities are severely limited compared to a designated terrorist organization, in terms of manpower, labor, and finances. Thus, a threat coming from a designated terrorist organization to shut down the entire electrical grid of Texas would be given great weight to its effectiveness.

The final question discusses, specifically, when will the threat be carried out. This threat was received in the morning, with the promise that the threat would be carried out in the next 24 hours. Therefore, it is likely to occur very soon. Overall, the analysis of the effectiveness of the threat is fairly straightforward, resulting in a dire need to have an effective cybersecurity counterterrorism model already in place to combat the existing threat. Thus, now that the questions have been answered, the final component is to place the threat on an imminence continuum.

As stated above, the imminence continuum has four major benchmarks: imminent, foreseeable, long-range, and uncertain. As we walked through the questions above, it is clear that this specific threat is imminent. The above exercise demonstrates the application of the questions necessary to evaluate the threat, and understand the need for a preexisting cybersecurity counterterrorism policy before such threat occurs.

INTERNATIONAL COOPERATION

U.S. policy-makers must determine whether cybersecurity policy will be *American centric* or will reflect significant, sustained, and institutionalized cooperation with like-minded allies. The answer to this question depends on assessing the extent to which cybersecurity poses a threat to the U.S. national security and public order. The possible impact on both requires that (in the American paradigm) both national security and law enforcement officials have a seat at the table of *cyber response*. Coincidentally, the existence of the cyber discussion with the U.S. national security demonstrates the effectiveness of cyber attacks.

It said that a word of caution is in order. Before allocating significant resources and determining asset allocation, it is necessary to determine whether cyber attacks pose a long-term, sustained threat defined as *grave and egregious*. Or, is it possible that cybersecurity is a *passing fad* that needs to be perceived from a transitory perspective, and that the threat has been exaggerated by interested parties with a vested financial interest in *hyping* the threat? The word of caution is not intended casually. The consequences of determining the threat are strategic, rather than merely tactical, and have significant ramifications, including economic implications, international agreements, impacting resource allocation (often resulting in resource-misallocation), and enhancing vulnerability posed by physical threats.

Forging international cooperation

The first step to effective international cooperation in cybersecurity is to forge lasting international partnerships with different countries and multistate organizations such as the E.U. The United States must strive to continue positive trade relations with different countries, as trade is vital to security. In order to promote true, effective partnerships, the United States must maintain open communication with liaisons between partner countries and organizations. Partner countries and organizations should speak through liaisons from counterpart agencies, departments, and organization (such as the Red Cross) from each country or multistate organization to ensure active communication about security and threat assessment and to promote effective use of international cooperation in counterterrorism.

VIGNETTE

Consider previous examples: Say a cyber attacker takes control of an air traffic control tower, but instead of Detroit, at London Heathrow Airport. Specifically, the air traffic control tower specifically being manipulated only directs international flights, flying to various countries in Europe, the United States, and Africa. Thus, the effectiveness of a cybersecurity policy would be greatly limited, were it not for international cooperation.

If there was a lack of international cooperation, the likely response would be each country attempting to implement their own, personal policy, without consulting the other and all the while interfering with the other. This greatly limits the effectiveness of a cybersecurity policy.

Now, imagine the same scenario, however a similar instance has been discussed previously, and there is a joint agreement among the majority of countries on best practices for responding to a cyber attack and assigned duties and obligations for any country that is involved. Which scenario would be more effective? I believe it is an easy answer.

Intelligence sharing

It is essential to promote active, effective sharing of necessary intelligence to those individuals with a need to know—to those individuals specified as intelligence liaisons within the greater coordinated international security plan (outlined below). Particularly, there must be international cooperation in sharing information vital to travel security, such as watch lists that outline some known threats to homeland security.

To the extent possible, countries should share intelligence about possible threats or intelligence about threats unknown to some countries whereas known to others, in order to promote international cooperation in threat assessment. There must also be intelligence sharing to ensure effective border security in order to have international enforcement of secured borders.

In addition, other nations could integrate the U.S. intelligence products with their own in efforts to identify, disrupt, and prevent terrorist attacks and activities on their own soil. Finding ways for the United States to share intelligence with other nations will create opportunities for the United States to receive and integrate intelligence products from other nations.

VIGNETTE

This continues with the earlier example. Imagine at London Heathrow, a cyber attacker has taken control of the air traffic control tower. Many international flights are now at risk, and citizens from over 50 countries are instantly in danger. Thus, it would seem that over 50 countries would like to be involved in the peaceful resolution of the scenario. Imagine further, not only the United States is using all the intelligence capabilities at their disposal, but also each of the countries implicated is contributing theirs as well.

The imagery is poignant. Now, instead of one country attempting to use its cyber capabilities against a cyber attacker, the power of over 50 countries is brought together against the individual cyber attacker. It would seem to be a no-brainer.

Now, let us consider another example. The underground train station, the Tube, in London was recently compromised. Cyber attackers gained access and managed to control several trains— affecting their abilities to start, stop, and open or close doors. Being a new situation in London, the English government is at a standstill for the best way to manage the situation.

On the contrary, imagine the exact same thing happened earlier this year in Washington. Cyber attackers, unfortunately, gained access to the Washington Metro system and were able to manipulate the trains, much the same way as done in London. Thus, it would seem an easy question, that Washington should share their lessons they learned from the situation to those being affected in London. Especially, Washington has just gone through it and may be able to minimize the damage affected against the English.

Not only should countries share intelligence about potential threats, or current watch lists, they should also share intelligence about past threats, and the responses that failed them, as well as the responses that helped them.

Coordinated international security plan

Partner countries must work together to develop a coordinated international security plan. This plan must outline steps for coordinated travel security, border security, and for determining and acting on known and unknown threats. Partner countries must communicate the possible threats to travel security and must create a set plan of action for disaster, terrorist attack, and terror threat scenarios. The plan should outline each multistate organization's/country's role within the greater security plan. The plan should articulate the coordination of country-specific agencies, departments, and organizations and outline how each entity must act in the face of a terror threat. A coordinated plan is vital to effective international cooperation in homeland security.

Joint training exercises

Fourth, partner countries must work together to create and undergo international training and simulation procedures. Representatives from partner countries must take steps to undergo specific disaster, terror attack scenario training, and simulation to ensure that each member follows the articulated security plan. Further, the training must ensure that each partner country follows the plan within its country, and also that the coordinated plan is followed among all the member countries as well.

Institutionalized continuity

The United States and its international partners must ensure institutionalized continuity both between nation leaders and each nation's key agencies and department liaisons. *Institutionalized continuity* on an international level refers to the idea that there must be a set process for which to continue, to pass on, the articulated security plan from one nation leader to the next. Each leader, liaison, representative, must ensure that they understand the coordinated security plan and must continue to improve the technology, intelligence, and training in order not only to develop but also to maintain a high level of international security.

This requires a dialogue between partner nations to ask, does the security strategy work? It requires the creation and continuity of parameters by which to measure international effectiveness. What is the ultimate goal, what are the expectations as to security training and financial ability? Ultimately, there must be an articulated, institutionalized plan to ensure the continuity of security between nation leaders, and all agency/department counterparts in order to promote effective international cooperation and ensure an effective homeland security strategy.

VIGNETTE

This prong emphasizes the goal articulated in previous examples. Institutionalized continuity is necessary in cyber, just as it is necessary in other aspects of life. Imagine you are traveling on a road trip. As you cross state lines—you are immediately pulled over. You were not going over the speed limit, you were staying in your lane, and all your headlights and brake lights were working properly. The officer approaches the car and simply asks, "Do you know why you were pulled over?" Dumbfounded, you respond, "No."

The officer response is simple, in this state, the laws are reversed and the cars drive on the left side of the road, instead of the right; therefore, with your driving on the right side of the road, you created an incredible danger against fellow motorists and must be written a traffic ticket. This seems preposterous, right? How could it be that from one state to the next, cars drive on the different side of the road? How can you remember which side is which? The distinction is critical because driving on the wrong side of the road likely will result in a serious accident.

This demonstrates the need for institutionalized continuity. Just like continuity is necessary in the rules of the road, continuity is necessary in the realm of cyber. And this continuity must continue throughout the United States and with other countries. Without it, countries will constantly be behind in their counterterrorism cybersecurity policy.

PRIVACY

All of us communicate with friends, colleagues, and family, in the United States and abroad. We do so through the Internet, through cell phones, and land lines. We are engaged in constant interaction with other. We do so with the understanding that privacy is increasingly becoming a quaint concept. As has been repeatedly reported, the National Security Administration is clearly monitoring phone conversations seeking to preemptively prevent acts of terrorism. The question is whether conversations are solely and exclusively monitored for legitimate national security purposes. The concern is that legitimate—and understandable—efforts are zealously conducted resulting in a net cast, so broad unrelated conversations are regularly monitored. In speaking with U.S. subject matter experts, it is clear that millions of phone conversations are listened to and monitored. The protection, I have been assured, is that intelligence community monitor is trained to stop listening once clear the conversation is unrelated to national security. Various senior officials have told me this on a number of occasions. I believe the intent was to reassure that conversations unrelated to national security are not monitored and privacy—in the context of surveillance—is protected.

Efforts aside, I find such conversations disturbing for two reasons, which are shown in Figure 5.3.

Admittedly, in the age of super sophisticated surveillance technology, the reasonable expectation of privacy has been significantly minimized (Figure 5.4).

Cyber, and cybersecurity, more than anything else, accentuates, exacerbates, and highlights the powerful tension between the right to privacy and the obligation to protecting national security. While we, *perhaps*, reasonably expect protection of privacy within the proverbial four walls of our home, that expectation is significantly minimized when engaged in the public sphere. What significantly complicates the present day paradigm is the obvious morphing between public and private because of social media. The importance and relevance of this to cybersecurity must not be minimized.

The reality is neatly summarized as follows: The moment an individual engages in electronic discussion, that interaction is in the public sphere.

- When told that monitoring for purposes of national security is *broad*, my skeptical ears and antenna are on "full alert"; I am deeply concerned that *national security is broadly defined*, which directly suggests cybersecurity policy is broadly defined.
- Broadly defining cybersecurity opens the door to *wide-scale surveillance resulting* in casting a wide net, thereby clearly impacting the individual's right to privacy.

Figure 5.3 Reasons.

Privacy standards
- *Katz versus United States*: Fourth amendment protects reasonable expectation of privacy that society is prepared to recognize, as objectively reasonable protection extends to person, not place
  In its application, court emphasizes *reasonable expectation of privacy*
- *Universal declaration of human rights*: No one shall be subjected to arbitrary interference with privacy, family, home, or correspondence...
- *International covenant on civil and political rights*: No one shall be subjected to arbitrary or unlawful interference with privacy, family, home, or correspondence...

Figure 5.4 Privacy standards.

Avid Facebook users tell me both a *private page* or a *public page* is available. However, even if the user chooses a private page, the average Facebook user has 600 friends. So if a user has 600 friends, to assume that all private friends would keep information private is illusionary, at best. In the context of cyber, the critical *delta* is the private–public morph, and the extent to which information is, truly, *not* protected. In developing a cyber policy, the extent to which *privacy has been minimized* is an essential piece of a very complicated jigsaw puzzle.

VIGNETTE

This discussion, the tolerance individuals have for foregoing privacy in terms of national security, was discussed earlier in the debate between Apple and the FBI over the San Bernardino shooter's phone. Are individuals willing to give *backdoor* access to the government in the name of protection? Are individuals who are open on their social media more willing to give government access, or do they feel a sense of privacy, despite their openness on social media? The difficulty lies in the end goal. In addition, whether that end goal is altruistic, can that be twisted if it falls into the hands of an individual who is not as altruistic?

This is an argument used against the idea of Apple creating a *backdoor*. If it creates such an operating system, the likelihood that it could fall into the hands of an individual with nefarious purposes exists, and that is a threat many Americans cannot accept.

The essence of the privacy-national security debate is balancing. Balancing is an imperfect equation reflecting both the reality of constantly moving threats and the never-ending efforts of cyber attackers to enhance their range, scope, and abilities. The seeming relentlessness of cyber attackers—large and small, domestic and international—raises powerful questions regarding both the effectiveness of countercyber policy and the extent to which society is willing to tolerate invasions of privacy. The balancing equation is hampered by a troubling sense that national decision-makers are consistently *taken by surprise*, when hackers successfully penetrate firewalls considered otherwise secure.

In part because I served as the Legal Advisor to the Israel Defense Forces, Home Front Command,* a U.S. Congressional Task Force (2008–2009) tasked with developing U.S. Homeland Security policy named me its Legal Advisor. My appointment included testimony before the Committee of Homeland Security, subcommittee on Intelligence, Information Sharing, and Terrorism Risk Assessment. My assessments can be summarized as given in Figure 5.5.

With respect to developing national cybersecurity policy, the primary question is how much imposition in the name of national security are individuals and the public willing to tolerate? The question is uncomfortable: At its core, it *demands resolution of the nature of the individual's relationship with the state.* Cybersecurity policy is dependent on successfully addressing this question that, undoubtedly, extends well beyond the Internet, national security, and privacy. From an existential and practical perspective, answering the question demands probing the social contract dilemma: to whom does the state owe a duty?

- A failure by the Bush administration and Congress to develop, much less articulate, a cohesive, coherent, and sustainable homeland security policy
- A failure to understand and conceptualize future threats; the age-old adage regarding generals who *fight yesterday's war* is applicable
- An unwillingness to define terms, thereby limiting state power and enhancing individual rights

---

Figure 5.5 Committee assessments.

---

* A position akin to Office of Legal Counsel, U.S. Department of Homeland Security.

But in terms of policy, we need to ask ourselves whether we as a society, corporation, and the government need to be much more Proactive in terms of imposing the requirement to create and implement protective measures. This to me is an inherent part of the policy discussion that emphasizes the requirement to understand the threat, recognize the threat, articulate the threat, and ultimately put in place protective measures against that threat. These measures are undertaken with the caveat that protective measures are not 100% effective. These realities—perhaps uncomfortable—require government to come before the public and explain *the inherent limits of cybersecurity policy* (Figure 5.6).

The questions that are to be considered in reviewing Chapter 5 are given in Figure 5.7.

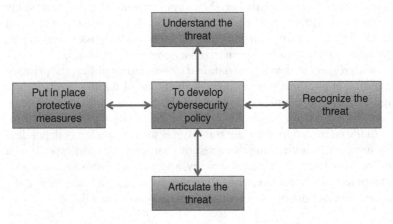

Figure 5.6 Cybersecurity policy.

- Is the working assumption that cyber attacks are inevitable?
- If cyber attacks are inevitable, how is that conveyed to the public?
- In respond to cybersecurity threats, should nation-states create a uniform policy?
- Should cybersecurity policy differ depending on if a nation-state or nonstate actor commits the attack?
- How should cybersecurity policy differ from policy regarding traditional armed attacks?

Figure 5.7 Review questions.

6 How do corporations respond to cybercrime?

INTRODUCTION

Corporations, large and small, are subject to hackers and are clearly being attacked, if not on a daily basis, very regularly. Some of the attacks are enormous, proportions affecting tens of millions of customers whose privacy is clearly violated. Their personal information is hacked; they are vulnerable, exposed, and concerned, if not angry. How corporations respond to cybersecurity is critical. The extraordinary importance cuts across tactical and strategic considerations. It is not an exaggeration to suggest that cyber threats are the primary focal point of corporations today. If they are not, then that reflects a serious misreading of a clear and present danger. That danger—palpable to the most casual observer—is indisputable.

However, clarity does not equate action; articulating threat recognition does not necessarily translate into concrete measures. There are, unfortunately, risks in acknowledging the threat; recognition of vulnerability can have significant financial consequences. While arguably understandable, stated and unstated concerns regarding acknowledging vulnerability are self-defeating and profoundly counterproductive. It is akin to the proverbial *head in the sand* approach, which reflects willful ignorance that conjures up the *monkey rule* of see no evil, hear no evil.

VIGNETTE

Consider the following: What constitutes a cyber attack against a corporation? In addition, what level of protection would you, as a consumer at a corporation, expect to exist in terms of protecting your privacy?

Many of us operate in a pattern—we frequent the same gas stations, grocery stores, and movie theaters. Assume for a moment that you are the type of individual who greatly enjoys going to movies, so much so that you attend at least once a week. Each time you attend a movie, you swipe your credit card to pay for tickets and concessions. What protection do you expect the movie theater to have in storing the credit card information? Is it similar protection you would expect the grocery store to have? Is it similar protection you would expect a financial institution, such as a bank, to have?

Now, consider your hospital system. Imagine you must go to the hospital quite frequently. You struggle with a chronic illness that forces you to go to monthly checkups. Also, imagine this illness is one that most do not know about, specifically your employer, and one you would like to keep private. This hospital record system has records of your medical history and payment information. What protection do you expect the hospital system to have in storing the medical records? Is it the same amount of protection you would expect them to have in storing your credit card information? Is that protection greater or smaller than the protection you would expect at the movie theater?

Finally, consider the types of response you would expect from both the movie theater and hospital system. It is likely you would expect additional response and recovery if the hospital system is breached versus the movie theater; seeing that at the movie theater, you simply lost credit card information.

REALITY AND ARTICULATING THREATS

The reality is that corporations are under attack daily and profoundly, with significant impact and consequences that are short term and long term. And yet, the clear—and disturbing—image is of corporate leaders expressing surprise in the aftermath of a successful cyber attack. The stock response of *we invested significant resources in protecting our clients and assets* is, at best, reflective of spin and damage control. It also suggests failure to recognize reality. The image of surprise is expressly compounded when recognizing that an attack on a corporation is seemingly an attack on the nation-state.

That failure, one assumes, is not predicated on the inability of corporate leaders to *understand* the existence of a clear danger. It does, however, suggest an unwillingness to *internalize* that danger. In practical terms, understanding does not equate internalizing; the former merely requires reading a newspaper, the latter demands concrete measures that require financial expenditures, resource allocation, and public acknowledgment of vulnerability. Even casual perusal of the Internet suggests that all three are an anathema to corporate leaders, regardless of location and size.

That approach is self-defeating, shortsighted, and counterproductive. It negatively impacts customers and investors; it imposes a burden on law enforcement; it affects other corporations and the general public. Perhaps most disturbingly—and significant—it emboldens cyber attackers who translate the failure of corporate leaders to openly address and acknowledge the reality of cyber attacks to weakness, if not incompetence.

The perceived incompetence is in failing to prevent attacks; the assumed weakness is in failing to acknowledge the threat. One of the primary *lessons learned* from my two decades' involvement in operational counterterrorism is the need—requirement is an apt term—for government to rationally and consistently articulate threats to society.

Articulation does not suggest fear; quite the opposite: It indicates the willingness to recognize and state the truth. That is a far more effective policy with respect to informing the public, directly interested parties, and actual and potential attackers.

VIGNETTE

Consider the benefit that comes from articulation of the threat. The following scenarios are, unfortunately, situations that occur daily throughout the country and that can be prevented if an articulation of the threat occurs beforehand, and action is taken to respond to such threat.

First, imagine an individual is walking down a back alley after leaving her night shift at a local restaurant. This particular area where the restaurant is located is in an area that is prone to violent attacks, specifically, many such attacks have already occurred in that specific alley. Now, imagine that two other individuals approach that individual—both are broad in statute and significantly larger than the individual leaving work down the back alley.

Watching this from a bird's-eye, the viewer would only assume the lone individual would come prepared, with a mechanism to deter such an attack, either pepper spray or mace. It seems difficult to comprehend why a lone individual would walk alone down a back alley late at night, specifically one where attacks have occurred previously, without some recognition of the need to carry a deterrent. The deterrent does not indicate a sign of weakness from that individual. Rather, it demonstrates an adequate articulation of the threat and recognition of the need to thwart a potential attack.

Second, imagine a person is logged into a public Wi-Fi connection, either at an airport or popular downtown café. With the bird's-eye view as used above, we can see that on the opposite side of the public Wi-Fi are hackers waiting for individuals to enter their credit card information. With this panoramic view, we are all too aware to stop the individuals from entering their credit card information and not let them fall prey to hackers.

Thus, with the articulation of the threat of hackers accessing credit card information, it does not make the individuals weaker. Rather, it emphasizes the need for articulation on actual, and perceived, threats and responding to them proportionally.

The third and final example involves hospital systems. At this day and age, several hospital systems have been hacked, either

(Continued)

with records being distributed or with the system being held hostage, until a certain ransom is paid. This is an occurrence that, unfortunately, has come to fruition several times. Thus, with the lone individual walking down an alley or individual using public Wi-Fi, it would seem the hospital system could learn from experiences of those before it and articulate such a threat and respond accordingly. However, this articulation is not happening among many corporations for whatever reason and must be addressed.

PARTNERSHIP

It represents a mature approach, signaling recognition of the threat, reflecting the undertaking of measures to minimize the threat, while not dismissing the possibility of an attack, nor understating its possible consequences and ramifications. In addition, it creates an environment where the customer is a *partner* in the context of counter cyberterrorism as the customer is treated as a *mature adult.*

The concept of *customer as partner* in combating cyberterrorism whereby a triangular relationship is created between the corporation and the client/customer—law enforcement is far more effective than unnecessarily minimizing—if not denying—the threat (Figure 6.1).

I write these lines sitting in a coffee shop in Jerusalem; the reality of life in Israel is that the public is a full partner with respect to counterterrorism. A suspicious package left unattended leads a concerned individual to call the police; entrance to a shopping mall is conditioned on passing through a metal detector; and school trips require accompaniment by an armed adult.

That is the reality. In the same vein—by analogy—the threat posed by cyber attacks requires corporations to form partnerships with customers and law enforcement. That partnership is, admittedly,

Figure 6.1 Triangular relationship with corporation.

burdensome; the burden is simultaneously existential and practical. It is, however, necessary. That, more than anything else, is the primary theme of this chapter: The threat of cyber attacks on corporations is undeniable; for minimizing this, the threat requires a concerted, direct, ongoing effort by those directly and indirectly impacted.

It is important to note that the effort is focused on *minimizing*, rather than *eradicating* the threat. Minimizing is within the realm of the possible; eradicating is an illusion and harboring that hope negatively impacts realistic efforts to minimize.

VIGNETTE

In responding to cybersecurity threats, it is easy to minimize the severity of the threat if one has not had personal experience with the ramifications of a cyber attack. Consider for a second that the following individual has never been a victim of identity theft. In addition, this individual has never even had his/her credit card hacked. This individual has never been victim of a corporate breach, resulting in his private information being published on the Internet. Overall, the individual has no experience with cybersecurity.

Now, consider an individual who has been a victim of identity theft, specifically his/her social security number was used to open numerous accounts, which resulted in the individual being unable to take out a loan because of their disastrous credit, all caused by the cyber attacker. It seems easy to assume that the individual who has experienced the severity of cyber attacks would be more inclined to minimizing the threat, because to them it is a rational, actual threat.

Let us consider the many things we currently do that are a result of an attack, a potential threat that was realized in an unfortunate way. For anyone who has flown recently, or in the last ten years, they are well aware of the security that one must go through to access their gate. Gone are the days of picking up loved ones at the gate—instead they have to wait outside security. Each individual must pass through a metal detector, and many are then additionally patted down. These efforts were implemented after 9/11—and became an expected part of traveling.

(Continued)

It is easy to make the argument that the security implementation likely would not have occurred but for the attacks on 9/11. The additional security, as well as locked pilot doors, was seen as a reaction to 9/11—and many, if not all, individuals understood their necessity. Now, let us go back to our comparison of the two individuals.

The person who has not had any experience with a cybersecurity attack would likely react the same as an individual who was not alive at the time of the 9/11 attacks. It would be conceptually difficult to articulate and realize such a foreign threat, especially if it has never happened to you. However, the individual who has been a victim of identity theft is much like the majority of the world who was alive during the 9/11 attacks. That individual clearly understands the severity of the threat and willingly articulates the threat in an effort to minimize it.

It must be a partnership in order for it to be effective. As seen in Figure 6.1, it requires cooperation between the corporation, the client/consumer, and law enforcement to effectively carry out a successful cybersecurity strategy.

STORY

A number of years ago, I worked with a major American corporation. To leadership's credit, a sophisticated simulation exercise was conducted. The stated purpose of the undertaking was to determine the company's points of vulnerability, with a particular emphasis on a localized act of terrorism. On the surface, the simulation was successful, so much so that at its conclusion, the chief executive officer (CEO) expressed his great satisfaction in a self-congratulatory moment. In doing so, he opened the door to criticism. One of the employees raised their hand and said, "we did the simulation and it was terrific, but we forgot this detail, and we forgot to address this potential event." The CEO said that "it's ok, we can manage that." But then, another employee raised his hand and said as a follow-up, "you forgot to address another detail."

Both points made by the separate employees addressed minor issues related to company protection and response; they were neither major nor catastrophic but rather small. Nevertheless, the CEO quickly realized a couple of things. One, he had prematurely engaged in self-congratulatory behavior. And two, if you are going to really engage in effective simulation exercises, cyber and otherwise, the devil is in the details. There is no substitute for thorough planning, realistic expectations, and honest self-assessment.

The CEO failed on all three counts; in particular, I was deeply troubled by unjustified self-confidence regarding the extent of corporate preparedness for all possible attacks. The takeaway—for me (hopefully for the CEO also)—was that in confronting cyber threats, corporate leadership needs to be much more self-aware regarding both the degree of threat and extent of *readiness either proactively or reactively.* This is particularly the case given the sophisticated nature of cyber attacks and the clear willingness of hackers to consistently engage in increasingly brazen attacks.

VIGNETTE

With the above story, the question becomes, what is the CEO's liability if he or she does not address the details that were forgotten in the simulation. If the details are acknowledged and undermined, and an incident occurs which comes at a significant cyber cost, can the CEO or corporation be liable, due to their awareness of the problem? In addition, should there be a legal responsibility that when a director is aware of an issue, they have a legal obligation to address the issue by a certain time period?

If not an enforceable legal obligation, is there a moral obligation? Either way, the question to consider is whether awareness of minor details that could result in significant cyber attacks results in increased liability for the corporation. If not, should it? The concern that comes with increasing liability is the corporation choosing to put its proverbial *head in the sand* to avoid liability rather than to become aware of problems.

A second story emphasizes a disturbing reality regarding the willingness—or more accurately unwillingness—of corporate leadership to *proactively address* the question of cybersecurity.

At a conference in the United States, I approached a vice president (VP) of security for a major U.S. corporation. We discussed the threat posed by cyber. It quickly became apparent that the two of us shared a common language and mutually recognized a glaring weakness. The VP, prior to joining the corporation, had served in law enforcement; based on our similar experiences and backgrounds, we agreed the corporation would greatly benefit from conducting sophisticated cyber simulation exercises that would demonstrate to senior leadership the points of weakness and vulnerability.

The VP was honest; his response was distressing. Although he well understood the enormous benefit to be accrued from such an undertaking, there was no doubt in his mind that the corporate CEO would adamantly oppose such an exercise. When I asked him why his CEO objects to the exercises, the answer was twofold. I think the gentleman was very honest: first, simulation exercises are time intensive and not inexpensive to conduct; second, if you conduct a simulation exercise and vulnerabilities are indicated, how will your shareholders respond? How will your competitors respond? How will hackers respond? In essence, he was telling me that the CEO preferred to put his head in the sand. I found that to be a recurring theme in talking to senior officials in corporations in the context of cyber. This reflects and articulates, actively and passively, a refusal to truly recognize the threat posed by cyber.

VIGNETTE

In considering the VP's response, the emphasis on his hesitation to act was on the expense to create such a simulation and the shareholder response. Are there potential ways to minimize or reduce either of those concerns. If such ways exist, who has the obligation to provide such a mechanism? In addition, who would be paying for that mechanism to be effective? If each of the VP's concerns were allayed, then, would his lack of response result in some form of liability?

Let us break each concern down and determine various ways to minimize both the economic and social costs to the VP and his corporation.

The first concern the VP emphasized is the economic expense— specifically that simulation exercises are time intensive and not inexpensive to conduct. Thus, what are some ways in which those costs could be minimized? Currently, in order to become

(Continued)

a corporation in America, it is required that individuals first file a certificate of incorporation, detailing its board of directors, general address, and other critical information.

This information is filed with the secretary of state. Now, consider, what if a training was then required for the incoming board of directors to engage in a simulated exercise for a response to a cyber attack. That would minimize the cost to the corporation, as it would be paid for by the secretary of state's office and would minimize the time spent later on in responding to potential, actual attacks.

However, the key difficulty in this option is the simulation would only apply to the incoming board of directors. And, as most of us know, often directors on boards are fluid, ever changing, and not consistent for long periods of time.

In response to the second concern, the VP emphasized a more social cost—concern of shareholder response. Demonstrating a corporation's weakness in terms of cybersecurity is not something a CEO or board of directors would necessarily want their shareholders to be aware of, specifically because it is simply showing the shareholders the company's greatest flaws.

However, there are two potential ways to allay this concern of negatively affecting the shareholders. The first way is to make such a simulation mandatory, pursuant to the rules of incorporation. Meaning, in order for a company to maintain its corporation status, they must comply with a mandatory simulation once every few years. This would even the playing field and force all corporations to engage in demonstrating their weaknesses, which would hopefully allay the shareholders of any one particular corporation, as they could see similar flaws in surrounding organizations.

The second way to minimize the social cost is by allowing such information to remain secret. This may logistically be more difficult, being that not much can be kept secret in our ever-globalized world, but it is an option that would not shock the shareholders as much as publicizing the information. Ultimately, with either option, the cost of negatively impacting the shareholders is minimized, whereas the awareness of necessity for cybersecurity protection is increased.

VULNERABILITY

In the context of threats posed by cyber, there are different vulnerability models that corporations can apply. I propose analyzing the relationship between corporations and cyber through a 12-point vulnerability model examining vulnerability from *beginning to completion of production.*

When focusing on product vulnerability to potential cyber attacks, corporate leadership must engage in rigorous self-assessment. Application of the 12-point *start to finish* model significantly facilitates assessing points of vulnerability. The effectiveness of this approach is enhanced when *resource prioritization and allocation* are included in the assessment. However, while identifying points of vulnerability is of utmost importance in developing a preemptive protection/preventive strategy, it is equally important to develop effective mechanisms whereby a cyber attack is quickly identified. Rearticulated preventive models are essential, but equally important are implementing measures by which a cyber penetration is quickly identified.

Innumerable attacks on corporations—small and large alike—have a troubling, recurring theme: the significant time that passes after the attack before corporations realize that a hack has occurred. This suggests a double-edged weakness as given in Figure 6.2.

The fact that an attack goes *unresponded* for a period of time enhances the vulnerability emanating from a single attack; from the perspective of a vulnerability continuum model, the unreported attack reflects continued vulnerability. Distinct from a traditional terrorism attack, which is predicated on a single attack reflecting a three-part model: *planning, implementation, conclusion,* as shown in Figure 6.3.

What is the risk in continuous vulnerability? It means that both present and future transactions are vulnerable, and existing and potential customers are at risk. The question is, how do corporations begin to respond? The question is posed with respect to *specific penetrations and general threats alike.*

- Firewalls are not sufficiently sophisticated to prevent an attack
- Firewalls are not sufficiently sophisticated to identify an attack, once it has occurred

---

Figure 6.2 Double-edged weaknesses.

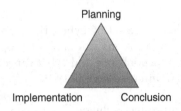

Figure 6.3 Three-part model.

However, before resolving those two questions, it is necessary to pose a preliminary question: Why are corporations so hesitant to be forthcoming in acknowledging that a *hack has occurred*? The easy answer is such an acknowledgment negatively impacts the corporation's financial stature, potentially deters new customers, gives competitors the opportunity to *score points*, and may convince existing customers to take their business elsewhere. That, more than anything, is what the VP for security was suggesting in our conversation. These concerns are understandable. They are, to a certain extent, defendable. They are also fundamentally misplaced.

VIGNETTE

As mentioned above, there is a clear distinction between traditional terrorism and the threat of a cyber attack. Traditional terrorism reflects a three-part model: planning, implementation, and conclusion. However, the threat of a cyber attack results in a corporation being continuously vulnerable. Thus, the question remains, how does one, or a corporation, remain constantly vigil against a continuous threat?

Consider running a marathon. In order to run a marathon, an individual must train. Maybe some could decide the day before to run a 5K, 10K, or half-marathon. Others would need sufficient time to train for those races. But a marathon is a race that most, if not all individuals, would need at least some time to train. And, in that training, the individual must remain constantly vigil. They must engage in runs during the week with a culminating long run on the weekends. They must eat right, sleep enough, and avoid injury as best as possible.

(Continued)

Protecting against a cyber attack is similar. Corporations eat right by taking care of their firewalls—ensuring their ability to thwart diseases (cyber attacks) or illnesses as best as they can. Corporations must do their best to avoid injury by checking on the firewalls intermittently to determine whether such a break has occurred. And finally, corporations must vigilantly train by engaging in simulations and exercises to visualize their weaknesses and address them. Ultimately, a corporation is constantly in marathon training when they are protecting against future cyber attacks.

LACK OF RESPONSE AND CANDOR

For a corporation, it is cheaper to react or handle a hack as opposed to spending money on defense and protection. The number of corporations who in the aftermath of a hack—successful or otherwise—come *forward immediately* and say "we've been hacked, we are vulnerable, let's learn from this" is minimal. That is a lost opportunity for both the company and others. It represents a double victory for the hackers: successful penetration and failure of corporations to learn from each other. Although each corporation has interests to protect, there are sufficient similarities and common values that would facilitate—and welcome—sharing information regarding successful or attempted penetration.

Nevertheless, the reality is that most corporations are extremely hesitant to come forward and acknowledge that they have been hacked. To that end, they are not forthcoming with customers, shareholders, and law enforcement. In addition, they are inhibiting or preventing other corporations from protecting themselves. Perhaps there is a shame element that despite enormous expenditures on firewalls and IT teams, vulnerability still exists. However, given the nefariousness of cyber attackers, and the damage caused, it would behoove corporations to put aside that shame factor and be much more forthcoming.

> *Let us consider customers*: As a customer of a company that has been hacked, you *immediately* want to know that your privacy is at risk. It is your right to know that *someone who*

you did not authorize is in possession of your social security number, your health information, and other information of a deeply personal nature. Corporations must have the *immediate* obligation to notify their customers.

Let us consider shareholders: Shareholders have significant financial interests at stake. That said, there are significant financial considerations in determining when—and how—to inform shareholders of an attempted or successful cyber attack. Clearly, corporations carefully weigh the impact of a negative response. Nevertheless, corporations must have the absolute responsibility to be as forthcoming as possible to shareholders and immediately.

Let us consider law enforcement: The faster the information is provided to law enforcement regarding a cyber attack, the more effectively the law enforcement can begin the process of identifying who is responsible. The attacked corporation, ostensibly, has a vested interest in assisting law enforcement; nevertheless repeated delays in reporting suggest conflict within corporations, regardless of ostensible benefits accruing from immediate reporting and information sharing.

VIGNETTE

Imagine the following scenario: You and your family recently spent a weekend away in Austin, Texas, staying at a popular hotel chain located downtown near Lady Bird Lake. While there, you enjoyed beautiful views from your hotel room and an overall wonderful stay. You paid with your credit card, without hesitation, and left great reviews on the hotel website. Later on that week, the hotel computer system is hacked, and your credit card information is now in the hands of the cyber attacker.

Imagine you are the customer. How soon would you like to know that the hotel system has been hacked, resulting in your credit card information being in the hands of a cyber attacker? Do you have a legal right to know? If the hotel delays telling you, do you suffer additional harm at the hands of the cyber attacker? What remedies are no longer available due to the hotel's delay in informing you of a cyber attack?

(Continued)

Ultimately, you, as the customer, would want to know immediately. Not just for the ability to respond effectively to the situation but also for the peace of mind knowing that your information is only in the hands of those you have entrusted. In this scenario, it is easy to comprehend why corporations, such as hotel systems, should have an obligation to immediately notify consumers of such a breach, specifically when it resulted in the loss of their private information.

Now, imagine you are a shareholder of the hotel chain. Would you want to know the hotel system suffered a cyber attack? By not notifying you as a shareholder, do you have greater confidence in the corporation? It would seem that the lack of notification to shareholders would result in increased distrust and animosity between the shareholders and the corporation, not the other way around. In today's world where cyber attacks are so sophisticated, and 100% prevention is next to impossible, it seems a shareholder would be more understanding of the hotel system suffering a cyber attack and immediately notifying them, as opposed to the hotel system suffering a cyber attack and trying to cover it up.

Finally, let us consider law enforcement. If we want law enforcement assistance in dealing with cyber protection, or expect their involvement, we cannot demand such a presence while delivering them such a lack of information. Law enforcement cannot be effective if they do not have the requisite tools at their disposal. Without promptly notifying law enforcement of a cyber attack, they are unable to *investigate the crime scene* and develop a patter—one in which they can warn and notify other hotel systems, or corporations, to be aware of. Ultimately, notification, of consumers, shareholders, and law enforcement, is essential.

To facilitate an *institutionalized reporting process*, we turn our attention to enhanced cooperation among parties that are directly affected by a cyber attack on a corporation.

COOPERATION—THE CONSEQUENCES
OF FAILING TO COOPERATE

Discussions with business leaders from different corporations highlight an intrinsic hesitation to share information with other corporations. On the one hand, this is understandable. Business considerations, financial interests, competition, and trade secrets are offered as primary reasons for such an approach. On the other hand, long-term strategic thinking suggests that a different approach is essential to successfully countering cyber attacks.

This long-term, more strategic approach is primarily predicated on the recognition of a *common enemy*, and *combining forces* will significantly enhance developing more effective countermeasures. The cooperation model suggests cooperation between corporations and between corporations and law enforcement.

An extensive phone interview with law enforcement officials in Florida highlighted the lack of cooperation on three distinct levels regarding cybersecurity: corporation to corporation, corporation to law enforcement, and law enforcement to law enforcement.

This is a good time to return to our previous discussion about Sony. When Sony was hacked, purportedly by North Korea, it is an indication of a major corporation being hacked. What could Sony have done proactively and reactively? I want to emphasize the significance of *threats, vulnerability, and timing*. So the easy answer in terms of proactive measures by Sony is to have invested additional resources, personnel, experience, and efforts in creating perhaps more sophisticated firewalls to better protect themselves. Perhaps, Sony did not fully appreciate their own vulnerability in accordance with the 12-point vulnerability model; perhaps, Sony officials were aware of their vulnerabilities but chose the *head in sand* approach. Or, perhaps, Sony underestimated the movie's impact from a North Korean perspective and failed to recognize the regime's cyber capabilities. The failing cuts across numerous vectors, including (1) lack of proactivity, (2) lack of recognition of someone else's abilities, and (3) lack of vulnerability recognition.

Here I want to interject a personal note from my own experience: *underestimating the capabilities, sophistication, and desires of attackers*, whether its traditional terrorists or nation-state or cyber, is an extraordinary mistake. Corporations, individuals, or nation-states, time after time, consistently underestimate the capabilities of potential attackers. We are dismissive; think our system is better or more effective or efficient. Successful attacks on corporations indicate and demonstrate, time after time, how leadership has failed to implement

- Conduct an honest assessment of damage done
- Take every measure to protect existing data
- As quickly as possible inform clients and customers
- Immediately inform law enforcement and work hand-in-hand with them to minimize the damage
- Inform the public
- Cooperate with other corporations both in order to minimize internal harm and to prevent future attacks

Figure 6.4 Corporation responses.

proactive preventive measures. The lack of institutionalized cooperation is both a manifestation and contributor to this disturbing reality. So, that is on the proactive end (Figure 6.4). What should corporations do upon discovering a penetration has occurred?

Undertaking these measures requires sophistication, teamwork, and an ability—and willingness—to analyze internal vulnerabilities. Immediate reactiveness minimizes future harm. However, the primary takeaway from examining how corporations react to successful hacking is a failure to respond quickly. Whether the failure to respond quickly is deliberate or not is an open question; nevertheless, it demonstrates clumsiness in not being able to identify the penetration quickly, and a failure to inform the customer.

The consequences are significant which are given in Figure 6.5.

Although focusing on possible lawsuits is understandable, the more important issues are the *failure to protect and the failure to inform*. The reasons are clear and are given in Figure 6.6.

What, then, does that mean for corporations? In stark terms, corporations need to be much more forthcoming. I think there are clear benefits accrued to a corporation in publicly discussing when it has been breached. Although the public will express concern in the

- Continued vulnerability
- Continued threat to customers
- Potential civil liability in the context of insufficiently protecting customer information/privacy and liability for failing to notify the customer of the breach and the consequences to the customer

Figure 6.5 Corporation consequences.

- Potential customers will hesitate to *bring their business*, once they discover failure to protect/failure to inform
- Existing customers may take their business elsewhere if they conclude all reasonable measures were not taken to protect their privacy
- The broader public will view the corporation negatively in the context of a failure to eliminate cyber attacks and minimize cyber risks, BUT the most powerful criticism will be *failure to tell the truth*

Figure 6.6 Failure points.

aftermath of a reported attack, the more long-term reaction will be an appreciation for *speaking the truth*. In addition, the knowledge of how a breach occurred, when shared with the public, could prevent a future breach in a different corporation in a similar manner. This change in behavior can have a large positive impact that could potentially affect millions of consumers.

That truth needs to address as given in Figure 6.7.

There is risk in this *open* approach; however, from a cost-benefit perspective, the *up-side* ultimately outweighs the *down-side*. Although an element of vulnerability results from openness and candor, an approach emphasizing implementation of measures to prevent future attacks, honesty with customers and the public reflects the following: (1) better customer protection, (2) better critical infrastructure protection; and (3) better protection of *larger interest*.

Risk mitigation predicated on honesty and proactive aggressive measures is a win–win. From a legal perspective, in terms of minimizing potential impacts of civil suits, a policy of candor and honesty predicated on "we are taking measures to minimize exposure of personal information and learning from it and working hand-in-hand with customers,"

- An acknowledgement of the penetration
- List of measures undertaken to immediately address the penetration intended to protect customers
- List of measures intended to protect customers in the future
- Reaching out to other corporations in the context of *information sharing*
- Implement aggressive countercyber measures

Figure 6.7 Corporation truth.

will mitigate the possibility of lawsuits against corporations. Such an approach indicates, from the corporation's perspective, a willingness to engage different audiences, particularly customers and law enforcement.

LAW ENFORCEMENT

There is no doubt in the fact that cyber attacks pose enormously difficult and new challenges to law enforcement. Conversations with law enforcement officials emphasize that cybercrime is profoundly distinct from both traditional *cops and robbers* and conventional terrorism. For law enforcement, cybercrime represents a distinctly different crime model posing complex and complicated challenges. Interaction with law enforcement officials suggests an enormous willingness to work closely with corporations both proactively and reactively.

The primary motivation is mitigating threats and minimizing the impact of an actual attack. The triangle of cybersecurity, corporations, and law enforcement demands operational capabilities that are, literally, developing as these lines are written (Figure 6.8).

For law enforcement to be able to effectively protect corporations, it requires a fundamental change in the context and concept of cooperation. For law enforcement to more effectively protect corporations, it will require corporations to be more forthcoming to law enforcement.

This cooperation will facilitate law enforcement's understanding of where the hack was, where the specific vulnerability was, and would enhance addressing the 12 points of vulnerability. This can only occur if corporations are much more forthcoming. In that sense, the burden is on them. The failure to work hand-in-hand with law enforcement prevents development—much less implementation—of a sophisticated, corporate-law enforcement cooperation model. Because of the vulnerability to individuals resulting from a successful cyber attack, there is a pressing need for *out of the box* approaches to law enforcement.

Figure 6.8 Cybersecurity triangle.

- Threat identification
- Vulnerability minimization
- Resource prioritization
- Cost–benefit analysis
- Asset protection
- Enhanced understanding of points of vulnerability
- Minimizing impact of future attacks

Figure 6.9 Law enforcement model.

However, the condition to that approach is the willingness of corporations to view law enforcement as full partners, both preemptively and reactively. To that end, a corporate governance model for cybersecurity is required; though presently untapped, the burden on its development rests with corporations. Law enforcement officials repeatedly articulated a willingness to closely work with corporations in its development and application. That model would emphasize the items listed in Figure 6.9.

INVESTMENT

Recent attacks have shown that it can take up to *243 days* for a corporation to understand, recognize, and discover that it has been breached. One of the reasons for this stunning—and deeply troubling—delay is that cyber prevent requires a significant investment. That investment is not only financial, it also requires an investment in personnel requiring an important shift in corporate culture requiring leadership to recognize and articulate cyber vulnerability.

In the context of vulnerability, the 12 production steps—sometimes referred to as *bean to cup*—require corporations, large, mid-size, and small, to ask themselves *to whom do they owe a primary duty*.

The obvious answers are shareholders and customers. The consequences are significant and expensive. That duty imposes on corporations the obligation to create sophisticated firewalls enhancing the protection owed to both audiences. However, in the context of prioritizing duty, I suggest the overarching duty is to the customer: the consequences of a breach to privacy are so daunting and significant that this duty imposes an *extraordinary obligation* on corporation leadership.

Understandably the cost question will be raised; corporate leaders, with whom I have met repeatedly, and emphatically, convey that concern. From their perspective, it is a justifiable concern. From a broader, more strategic concern, this perspective is not justified. Given the threat posed by cyber, corporations need to recognize the primacy of the duty owed to the customer rather than to the shareholder. That rearticulated prioritization model imposes on corporate leadership the requirement to be more forthcoming, honest, and candid even *if it* causes consternation among shareholders. This approach is premised on the recognition that the corporation's primary duty is to protect—and inform—the customer, even if that duty imposes a cost on the corporation.

Otherwise, customers can legitimately ask—Is the corporation sufficiently protecting me? If the answer is no, then that is extremely worrisome in the context of how corporations respond to cybersecurity.

Similarly, and no less importantly, sophisticated cooperation measures among corporations and law enforcement must be implemented. Although understandably problematic and perhaps a source of discomfort, the obligation to the customer warrants, if not demands, such an approach. Although some corporations have indeed begun the process of expending significant resources on cyber protection, these are but a handful of corporations.

Until all corporations—large, mid-size, and small—fully internalize the grave threat posed by hackers, counter cyber measures will fall short, thereby posing significant risks to hundreds of millions of customers. This in and of itself justifies development of a cyber policy predicated on informing the public, regardless of the costs, direct and indirect alike.

Direct costs include hiring expensive cyber experts; indirect costs include the possibility of losing business. Additional costs include loss of revenue, while cyber attacks are responded to. And there is a fourth cost: How do you maintain *customer loyalty* when not only has the corporation failed to protect the customer but has—perhaps more importantly—failed to notify/inform the customer of a cyber attack?

The best way to ensure my loyalty is to demonstrate to me that you have put into place proactively sufficient, satisfactorily, and sophisticated cyber protection measures that will protect me. If in the aftermath of a successful hack, it turns out that you did not sufficiently proactively protect me, then it is fair to assume that you will lose me as a customer. Conversely, if you being the corporation put into place these kinds of sophisticated firewalls and there is a hack, my assumption is that you will be less prone to lose my loyalty, because from my perspective you have undertaken measures to protect me and I fully know that you cannot protect me 100% of the time.

So while customer loyalty is mentioned as a cost, I think the truth of the matter is with respect to policy and corporations; the failure to put a plan in place is a sure way to lose customer loyalty than not putting a plan into place.

What does that mean in terms of geopolitics? Large corporations, international in orientation, regardless of where their headquarters are, have branches throughout the world. There is, obviously, a compelling link between geopolitics and corporations, particularly internationally focused corporations. This requires corporations, which have an international presence, to be fully cognizant of laws regarding cybersecurity obligations.

An American corporation considering establishing a presence in another country must fully understand cybersecurity laws to ensure that sufficient measures have been undertaken regarding compliance. In addition, corporations must expand significant energies in understanding different cultures. The implication is clear: If the host country is particularly sensitive to cyber attacks, both in terms of laws and culture, then the investing (external) corporation needs to not only ensure compliance with the laws but also with respect to the cyber culture and cyber protection culture of that country.

I want to relate to you a conversation or conversations that I have had with vice presidents for corporate security who are concerned that the C level is not sufficiently focused on cyber, but what I suggest is that we examine the sensitivity of American corporations that want to invest overseas; then the requirement, the compliance requirement, in terms of law, policy, and culture on an American corporation is significant. I would suggest in that context to minimize the possible threat posed by a cyber attack; that minimization is at the end of the day going to be a negative from the perspective of that corporation in terms of future clients and also in the context of shareholders.

So what do corporations need to do? Corporate leaders can sit around the table and have endless discussions about points of vulnerability, but the single most effective mechanism to truly understand those points of vulnerability is by conducting sophisticated simulation exercises either inhouse or with experts to identify where the corporation is vulnerable.

I would warmly recommend law enforcement to have a seat at the table along with other corporations and government officials. Otherwise, the exercise will be akin to an echo chamber, largely ineffective in terms of articulating and implementing an effective cyber security policy. I fully understand and respect that for many corporate leaders, the idea of institutionalized cooperation with law enforcement, government entities, other corporations, and competitors raises red flags.

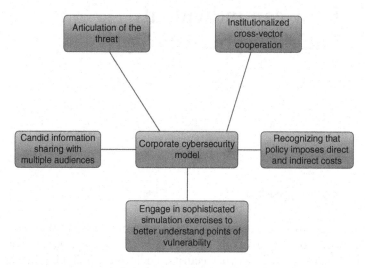

Figure 6.10 Corporate cybersecurity model.

- Should corporations be responsible for their own cybersecurity?
- Should the government force corporations to have cybersecurity policy?
- Should corporations be required to share relevant cybersecurity information with other corporations, including competitors?
- Should corporations be required to report when they have been attacked to law enforcement?
- Should corporations have a duty to report a cyber attack to shareholders?

Figure 6.11 Review questions.

However, given the cost, impact, and nefariousness of corporate security hackers, I do not believe that there is any alternative other than to rearticulate the corporate cybersecurity model (Figure 6.10).

The questions to be considered in reviewing Chapter 6 are given in Figure 6.11.

Further, after the discussion and considerations regarding corporations, it would be extremely beneficial to learn from a current, real-life scenario, as depicted in the CBS 60 Minutes episode entitled, *The Great Brain Robbery.*

---

* http://www.cbsnews.com/news/60-minutes-great-brain-robbery-china-cyber-espionage/.

7 How can individuals mitigate cybersecurity?

INTRODUCTION

Moving on from corporations, we next can consider who makes up corporations. Individuals can mitigate the threats, dangers, and vulnerabilities posed by cybersecurity. Each of us, individually, plays a role in the context of cybersecurity. Here is a small example. Many of us have been hacked, either our credit card is breached or our email is hacked. Thus, we each have personal experience. Cybersecurity can be viewed on both a personal and broad level.

CYBER ON A PERSONAL LEVEL

In our personal experiences, the initial reaction is irritation. However, irritation is typically the highest loss we suffer. In a credit card breach, the bank usually recoups the money, and the harm is not as significant. Overall, it is a financial short-term loss that is compensated, once funds are returned. Individually, a credit card breach once is not a blatant red flag. A second, or even third, credit card breach should raise a red flag about the need to better protect ourselves.

Most of us do not take sufficient protection, or meet minimum-security standards, to better protect our credit cards and passwords. Why is that? The reason being is that often there is little harm in a credit card breach, merely an inconvenience, so the threat of breach is not as intimidating. The ultimate question is whether or not minimizing the inconvenience is the appropriate individual response to a cyber attack and considering whether a credit card or password beach goes beyond irritation.

The notion behind minimizing the inconvenience seems to be an incorrect response. A hacker, attempting to breach into credit cards

---

- How do we better protect ourselves?
- What are our points of vulnerability?
- How great is the threat truly posed by cybersecurity?

Figure 7.1 Individual questions.

and passwords, would prefer each of us to minimize the inconvenience rather than address the threat.

The important questions each individual should ask are given in Figure 7.1.

In considering the points of vulnerability, the question becomes, should we have greater expectations or demands of our credit card companies to better protect us? As individuals, we seem to have the responsibility to better protect ourselves as the threat of a cyber hack is significant. As mentioned previously, cyber hacking does not necessarily result in deaths. However, our individual records will be exposed, and that results in a threat. Many past events demonstrate the loss that extends beyond credit card breach and loss of dollars.

VIGNETTE

As mentioned above, it is critical to consider the points of vulnerability in determining how best to protect ourselves against a credit card breach. The points of vulnerability analysis result in you, as an individual, examining facets of your life to determine the points of easiest penetration for the cyber attacker.

First, a cyber attack often occurs through email. Specifically, a cyber attacker gains access to our private email account, and in so doing, accesses a plethora of private information that you, as an individual, would rather keep private. Why does this occur? That question turns on passwords. How often do we change our password? How different is our email password from our passwords to other things? When we receive reminders to update our password, do we actually do it? Is our password something that can be easily guessed, either our maiden name or the city in which we live? All these considerations create a point of vulnerability.

(Continued)

Second, a cyber attack often occurs when such attackers access our credit card information. This can occur from entering our debit pin and a hacker obtaining that information. Like our email password, are we doing a sufficient job protecting our ATM password? The gas station I frequent regularly has a reminder every time I enter my pin to make sure that I *protect my pin*. The encouraged method is to place my hand over my other hand as I enter the pin, thus inhibiting the ability to view the pin. Do I do this every time? Not usually. I tend to get distracted or forget, despite the warning beforehand. This creates a point of vulnerability.

Third, a cyber attack can occur against us as an individual, when we are careless with our social security number. There are two ways we can be careless with our social security number, either by our own doing or by the doing of others. We can be careless, by our own doing, by entering our social security number onto websites that are not adequately protected. An instance that specifically affected one reader is when she was scouting for apartments on CraigsList. One posting required the individual to fill out information for a requisite background check, which included entering her social security number.

Without a second thought, this individual entered her social security number and submitted the information to the unknown website. This trick is one frequently used by cyber attackers and is an easy way for them to prey on the ignorant in accessing their social security numbers. This was a direct result from that individual's proactive entering of her social security number.

We can be careless with our social security number and be directly affected from the doing of others. Another individual frequented a local dog park. Around this dog park, there were signs that clearly said, "Take your belongings, hide your keys, and lock your car." Despite the warnings, this individual left her wallet on the front seat. Not only that, this individual left her social security card in that same wallet that was in the front seat. After finishing at the dog park, this individual came back to her vehicle to discover a shattered front window and a now missing wallet and social security number.

In order to better protect as individuals against cybersecurity attacks, it is critical to recognize the many points of vulnerability in our lives and determine ways to best minimize the risks created by each.

EXAMPLE: BREACH OF HEALTH RECORDS

Consider a breach of health records, consider your record, or your family member's records, exposed and made available to others. This breach would have dire consequences. If your records are exposed and disseminated on the Internet, there is a potential for embarrassment. We each have things within our medical records that we would prefer others not to know. Thus, a breach of such stature results in embarrassment from the dissemination of information meant to be confidential.

In addition to such breach affecting our personal lives, a breach of medical records may impact possible employment opportunity. Potential employers may, even through nefarious methods, inquire and obtain one's health record and ask additional questions in determining an employment opportunity. Not only potential employers, an exposure of confidential health records may affect your current employer. Let us take back and consider, for example, if at your current employment, certain medical records are revealed, it may impact the possibility of promotion, coworkers' perception, and your ability to continue to be an effective employee.

In addition to personal and employment relationships, such breach may affect your relationship with the insurance company. As we all are aware, when you seek health insurance, there may be things you do not want the insurance company to know. However, once the record has been breached and disseminated, that information is out there for all to see, including the insurance company.

Fourth, in addition to personal, business, and insurance relationships, the breach of health records may result in that dissemination of information on social media, specifically Facebook or Twitter. Thus, the breached information has now affected broad contours of your everyday life.

VIGNETTE

Consider the following real-life example. An individual is currently undergoing treatment for Stage IV esophageal cancer. She is enrolled in a clinical trial, which results in her going every other week for lab work and every other week for treatment. This individual is not currently employed, nor is her husband. However,

(Continued)

at her last treatment, the computer's system was down. Thus, an already long six-hour day turned into an even longer nine-hour day as the medical team tried to obtain the requisite blood work without access to a computer.

This delay resulted in additional sickness for the individual, as her body currently cannot handle too much strenuous activity, being that she is currently battling terminal cancer. However, the delay not only resulted in additional sickness, but it resulted in a fear of continuing treatment. At the time the computer system was down on the day of treatment, no one was aware the system was being hacked. Rather, they believed it was some form of malfunction.

However, five days later, the system was still down, and it was very clear that they had been a victim of a cyber attack. This particular individual is not fearful of her medical records being exposed to current or future employers, nor is she fearful of the records being posted on social media. Rather, she is most fearful of the inability to access the requisite clinical trial treatment due to such a cyber attack. This clearly demonstrates that a breach of a hospital system has multiple negative consequences; thus the need for prevention and protection is clear.

KEYS TO PROTECTION

The threat has been demonstrated. The harm has been demonstrated. Therefore, the question becomes, what is there to do? The first key to protection is education of individuals. It is critical to educate the individual about the dangers posed by cyber hackers. The second key to protection is educating the individual in the steps to pressure their bank, their health providers, their insurance companies, and other holders of confidential information to engage in more sophisticated and effective protection of the individual.

The two keys to protection, individual education on protection and individuals demanding protection, create a two-way street.

When we, as the individual, sign up with a health care provider, many of us do not sufficiently demand the insurer to demonstrate how they will go about protecting our records. This is a mistake. It is reasonable, as an individual, to demand the health insurer to be proactive in terms of minimizing each individual's vulnerability to cyber attack.

This can be seen as a form of cyber hygiene, a mechanism, or infrastructure to consistently address adequate protection. This burden falls on two groups, as demonstrated in the two-way street above. The first burden is on the individual in terms of how I, as the individual, protect myself. These protections are as simple as changing a password on a regular basis. In addition, the individual can, and arguably should, take the next step to demanding, not only more of itself but of the services rendered to them.

Here is an example for the second key to protection. If the individual buys something from the health industry, they can supply a list of demands. In terms of cyber protection, the demand is to see a game plan, a checklist of sorts, on how the company will protect the confidential health records they are entrusted with. This includes a minimization of a threat of hack by identifying points of vulnerability.

This relates back to a previous chapter involving how corporations respond to cybersecurity. In that chapter, we discussed the argument that corporations must be more forthcoming when they suffer a cyber attack. This forthcoming nature must not only apply to law enforcement, for the purposes of enhancing cyber protection, but also to the individual consumer, for the purpose of relaying the extent and severity of the hack. There is a direct link between the responsibility and expectations we have with corporations to the responsibility and expectations we have with health insurers, being that both are holders of individuals' confidential information.

VIGNETTE

In continuing with the earlier example of the cyber attacker focusing on the computer system of a clinical trial, let us apply the two-way street diagram to see how protection can be attained, both by individual education on protection and individual demanding protection. Individual education on protection focuses on the little things that individuals can do to ensure protection. Individual demanding protection focuses on the demands an individual should make to those who are storing the individual's information.

With the example earlier, an individual is currently undergoing treatment at a local clinical trial. One day, the computer systems were attacked, resulting in that day's treatment being extended

(Continued)

significantly, as well as the actual threat of the treatment not being able to continue due to lack of control over the computer system.

In considering the first prong, individual education on protection, it is critical to determine in what ways the individual could actually educate themselves. This is difficult in this particular scenario, because there is not much the individual has control over with the clinical trials computer system. They do not use a login; therefore, it does not deal with a necessity of a changed password. In addition, they have not been reckless with their information; rather, they have entrusted it with the clinical trial organizer, in the understanding that the information will be protected. Thus, in this scenario, the two-way street focuses more on the individual's need to demand protection.

The question then becomes how can an individual demand the clinical trial operators to protect their critical information. When initially consulting with the clinical trial, did the individual ask what protection was currently in place for their private information? Did they demand any sort of mechanism to be in place before they shared personal information? Did they expect the organization to react in a certain way in the event of an attack?

Unfortunately, in a situation such as this one, where the individual is battling Stage IV esophageal cancer which has been deemed terminal, the individual does not have many options for treatment. Thus, this clinical trial, despite its potential lack of protection of its personal information, might still be its only option. Therefore, its ability to adequately demand such protection may be limited due to its required nature.

Either way, it is critical for individuals to recognize the two-way street. Thus, not only there is a need for individuals to educate themselves on protection, but also there is a comparable need for individuals to demand such protection. As seen in the earlier corporations' chapter, corporations can be hesitant to provide adequate protection or report actual instances of attacks. Thus, without the two-way street mechanism and the individual taking the initiative to demand such protection and education, many businesses or organizations would fall significantly short of the barometer they should be required to reach when storing personal information.

INDIVIDUAL PROTECTION DEMANDED
OF HEALTH INSURERS

Let us walk through an example. At one point, I injured myself and went to the doctor. After that visit, I gave them a credit card to pay for the services provided. I provided all the information inquired about my health records and social records. I answered each question in good faith as I assumed the questions were being asked in good faith. It is important for the physician to access the information, so he can better treat me. Thus, it is not only in my best interest to answer the questions in good faith, but it is also in his best interest to ask the questions in good faith. This will allow the visit to be more effective and more beneficial to my health.

As I answered the questions, the physician entered all the information electronically, whether it is in a desktop computer, tablet, or laptop. The question then became—where does this information go? Is my personal, confidential medical history protected? Is this information held in a vault only accessible by password? Or, are the records not fully protected? Is that information now available to any person with a computer who has the ability to hack?

Consider, when we answer the physician's questions in good faith, we assume they are asking because they need an answer. We assume that information is critical to the ability to successfully treat us. It rarely occurs to us to consider where the information could end up. Confidential medical records are potentially a *low-hanging fruit*, because the record production is essential in the medical field and becomes an opportunity for hacking.

However, let us pause and evaluate what would occur if I did not answer the questions in good faith. If I were to pause and refuse to answer, it would make it increasingly more difficult for the physician to treat me effectively. At that point, the physician would have an incomplete history, which significantly hinders his professional ability to provide necessary medical assistance.

Thus, there is complexity in not answering the questions. By not answering the question, to avoid a record being made public, it has the potential to cause harm in the present medical issue. On the one hand, there exists a societal expectation that when we go to the physician for assistance, certain questions are asked, and we must answer to allow them to treat us more efficiently and effectively. This information, inevitably, is entered into an electronic device and stored as such.

So, what if you have something to hide? What if there is something in your personal history that you did not want to share with others? What if you were convinced that the information given in the physician's questions was going to be victim to a cyber hack? Does that mean, as an individual fearing a potential cyber attack, you should not cooperate with the physician's questions? The answer may be yes. But, that is not very realistic. In the context of the way we share information, the reality is we make ourselves vulnerable quite frequently. And in doing so, we expect our information to be protected.

The reality is that information is likely never fully protected. The information that we consider private and confidential is likely not protected to the extent we may like it to be protected. The question then becomes, how do we go about more effectively protecting ourselves as individuals? And as such, what potential remedies are there in the event of a cyber attack?

VIGNETTE

As seen in the above discussion, many times we are obligated to respond to personal questions, to better ourselves physically, and in so doing, we place our information at risk of a cyber attack. However, as also mentioned above, the need to disclose critical information to our health care provider often outweighs the fear of our information being exposed. But, consider the following, what if your personal information is exposed to your current employer?

Imagine you work in a manual labor position. This position requires you to often lift things over 75 pounds or more. Thus, there are straight height, weight, and fitness requirements to be eligible for the job. You have easily passed these requirements. You are in the requisite height and weight and maintained yourself in excellent physical shape. Therefore, you have secured the job, and you are a stellar employee.

Now, imagine, despite your current ability to pass the height, weight, and fitness requirements, there was a time in your past where you were unable. Imagine you dealt with an illness that inhibited your fitness ability and there was something that had the threat of reoccurring again. If your employer knew this information, it might disqualify you from employment, simply due to the employer's fear of potential relapse.

(Continued)

Therefore, you have chosen, as it is your right, to keep your personal information to yourself. And, since you passed the height, weight, and fitness tests with flying colors, you are now happily employed in this manual labor position. However, on this day, your previous health physician's office was breached. A cyber attacker, who then accessed all the personal medical records that were on file, penetrated the computer system.

This attacker published the medical information on an easily accessible site, allowing all to view private medical records. Not only was the medical information posted, but also it was directly associated with the pertinent individual, making it very specific as to which records belonged to whom. At this point, the employer became aware of the breach and the visible public records, and went on to determine if any of his employees were affected by the cyber attack.

The employer of the individual in the manual labor position now realizes that his employee, despite passing the height, weight, and fitness requirement with flying colors, has dealt with an illness that is likely to relapse, and one that can be triggered by lifting heavy things. Therefore, in order to avoid any future injury or liability for the employee, the employer promptly fires the employee.

Now, seeing that the employee has done no wrong and should be eligible for the position, how could the employee have acted differently to avoid this result? If the employee had not been forthright with his physician originally, he might never have recovered from his illness. Had he withheld information in the fear of termination from a future employer? It is likely that his current illness would have continued for a much longer time. Therefore, it seems apparent, that withholding information is never the answer.

The question then turns to whether or not the employer can lawfully fire that individual due to his/her learning of information from breached records. It seems unfair that the employer can access that information, even though they were not the ones who originally committed the cyber attack and posted the documents. This discussion comes at a later time in determining liability for those who access the information that was unlawfully siphoned from a rightful organization.

REACTIONS AND REMEDIES TO A CYBER ATTACK

Consider the following: If your personal bank account is hacked, the first thing you do is call the bank and clarify which purchases were yours, which were not, and the money that was stolen is returned to you. Rarely do we then ask, is there someone I can sue? This raises an interesting question. Who would you sue? The bank? The credit card company? To both, the answer seems to be no. Both the bank and the credit card company have protections installed to protect themselves from the individual.

So, can you sue the individual who caused the breach? Are there penalties against a cyber hacker? Potentially, if law enforcement and corporations are working together, there can be penalties. This relates back to previous chapters where we considered the responsibilities and complexities of law enforcement and cyber attacks, as well as corporations and cyber attacks. It is critical for the two to interact. In so doing, the identification of a cyber hacker is made easier. However there likely is no one to sue, because the hacker's identity is protected through various firewalls. Thus, the remedy cannot be a lawsuit but simply recouping our losses.

Now, take for example, your information is hacked, and someone else disseminates that information. Can the disseminator be sued in a civil suit? The argument is yes; if you can identify who indeed has caused you the harm, it is legally feasible. However, is it realistically feasible? At this moment, the answer is likely no. The energy required to identify the hacker, or the disseminator, is something the average individual does not have the resources, time, or knowledge to accomplish.

To emphasize, the disseminator of hacked information is just as nefarious as the individual hacking. They both caused harm to the individual. It is critical to not minimize the harm, specifically in the context we have been speaking, of health records.

INDIVIDUAL PROTECTION

What is the incentive for protection? How do we go about developing more effective protection?

A few guidelines are given in Figure 7.2.

In regards to the last item, when purchasing items online, do not supply your social security information. Only supply your social security number by phone. Understand that once you put your social security number online, it is out there. In addition, be cognizant of the

- Create new and innovative passwords regularly
- Change your passwords often
- Do not share your passwords with others
- If written or recorded, destroy the paper they are recorded on or preserve it in a safe location
- Be more demanding of corporations or businesses with whom you provide specific information
- Be smart in the way you share information

Figure 7.2 Individual guidelines.

vulnerabilities. In doing so, be demanding of determining ways to protect those vulnerabilities. In recognizing the vulnerabilities, this is best done by making such concerns an act of daily discussion with friends, families, and coworkers. Understand the reality that vulnerabilities exist. The threat of cyber is most poignant, not in terms of physical loss, but in terms of financial loss, embarrassment, or pain in items made public.

In being more aware and cognizant, it is critical for individuals to recognize that we are all vulnerable to attacks in many ways that are not often discussed. Further, any priority asset that is not given sufficient protection can be considered vulnerable. The key is to recognize that confidential information may be disseminated. If you want to avoid dissemination, it is critical to assume responsibility for more effective protection. As stated in the previous chapter, the responsibility lays with the corporation. In addition, the individual must assume accountability and demand additional protection.

VIGNETTE

There are many instances, just existing in the world we do, assuming accountability and demanding additional protection are just not the options. Many employers require specific information when beginning employment. This information can range from social security numbers, health records, criminal records, and other important documents. One does not have the ability to simply deny the employer access to these forms. In so doing, the individual would lose the opportunity to potentially work for the employer.

(Continued)

The question becomes, if I want to work for a specific corporation, but I am fearful of their ability to maintain confidentiality with my records, how do I demand adequate protection? Will demanding such protection cost me a potential job? Even if such protection is demanded, will the company respond and supply the protection? Does such absolute and adequate protection even exist?

Overall, it is increasingly more difficult for an individual to be personally accountable. As mentioned earlier with the Apple/FBI dispute, the FBI wants to access the phone to gain access to personal information. This information is also stored on the Cloud. There is a plethora of documents stored on the Cloud that individuals would prefer to be kept private. Thus, those individuals demand accountability by the corporation to keep them private. However, many cyber attackers can bypass firewalls despite their best attempts. Thus, the difficulty for an individual comes as the cost of demanding adequate protection from a corporation, coupled with the realization that adequate protection may not exist.

With personal accountability, the individual must pause and consider the websites they download information from, or supply information to. It is essential to be extremely cautious in terms of the information we provide to the Internet. Cyber hackers are more sophisticated than us, the average individual. They are capable of penetrating our closely held secrets, thus making us vulnerable. In that context, it would be beneficial to be more prepared to protect ourselves from future attacks.

We cannot live in a world where there is a rampant fear of putting anything on the Internet. It does not mean being 100% suspicious all the time. It just requires an additional realization about future attacks. In so doing, it allows the question to be asked, what will I do once I have been hacked? Responses can vary from giving out personal information less or giving out personal information in different ways.

CONCLUSION

Despite our attempts to be careful, many individuals fall prey to phishing and scams. Of those individuals, the majority are elderly. Thus, the younger generation has an obligation to educate themselves, their family members, and their neighbors to be smart on the Internet. Thus, the discussion on the individual comes with an obligation to share information with the understanding that by sharing we can, both individually and collectively, minimize the threat posed by cyber hackers.

The following are questions to consider in reviewing Chapter 7 (Figure 7.3).

- Should I protect myself from a cyber attack, or should the responsibility lay with the government?
- What protective measures can the state impose on the individual in cybersecurity protection?
- Should the individual bear responsibility when hacked?
- If no, what are the consequences of that?
- What is the individual's responsibility to report when hacked?

Figure 7.3 Review questions.

8 How does law enforcement mitigate cybersecurity?

INTRODUCTION

This chapter discusses the relationship between law enforcement and cybersecurity, specifically how law enforcement can more effectively work with corporations, individuals, and states to assist them in protecting from cyber attacks. The emphasis will be on what law enforcement can do to mitigate cybersecurity or cyber threats.

VIGNETTE

Before delving into the law enforcement discussion, let us first consider the role law enforcement plays in regard to the previous entities that we discussed. With corporations and law enforcement, there is a coexisting relationship, where each side leans on the other and requires their cooperation and assistance to be most effective. For law enforcement, they require the cooperation of corporations in reporting a cyber event and documenting it correctly.

Over the years, consider how law enforcement is able to improve. In solving intricate problems, such as cyber attacks, terrorism, or kidnappings, they are forced to develop a problem-solving technique. This may consist of community support, technological advancements, or door-to-door surveying. Either way, law enforcement has increased their capabilities as they develop patterns and trends of how best to respond to difficult situations. The same is true in the realm of cyber. In order for law enforcement to improve in their response to cyber, it requires corporation

(Continued)

cooperation to assist in the development of a response and pattern to effectively combat a cyber attack.

Similarly, we have previously discussed the effect of individuals. Not only does law enforcement rely on corporations in both thwarting and responding to a cyber attack but also on individuals. Before the latest technology advancements, law enforcement solely relied on human intelligence and observation to solve a crime. It required talking to many people, the cooperation of many, and the memory of many. Similarly, a cyber attack, although it may not require the cooperation of many or memory of many, requires the cooperation of at least some individuals.

Thus, law enforcement is the final prong or step in the cyber attack response. Law enforcement is the facet that steps in last, ultimately responding to the situation at hand and developing mechanisms to avoid it in the future. Unlike corporations, law enforcement personnel do have an obligation to act in a certain way or report a certain instance. In addition, it is, without a doubt, a valid fact that without the cooperation of corporations, individuals, or other entities, law enforcement would be nowhere as effective as it can be. This understanding furthers our analysis later in the chapter, as we decipher the responsibilities of law enforcement.

OBLIGATIONS AND RESPONSIBILITIES OF LAW ENFORCEMENT

The first question to ask is what obligations and responsibilities do law enforcement owe to individuals, states, and corporations? This is all speaking in terms of cyber. This is a practical question, as well as a broad philosophical point of inquiry. There are numerous ways to address this question. Historically as a society, we encouraged law enforcement to educate our children about the nefariousness of drug dealers or not getting into cars with strangers. We encourage law enforcement to warn us about the dangers posed by a variety of criminals. Why? Because, we want law enforcement to protect us as individuals.

Thus, the question of obligation and responsibility of law enforcement then becomes: Does law enforcement owe the same duty to an evolving threat of cyber? Even when the cyber threat is not defined, unclear where it originates from, what harm it can cause, and who is ultimately responsible? This is a complicated and controversial question. However, it is a question that must be discussed, and that discussion will encourage a step in the right direction.

Given the threat posed by cyber attacks, whether it is attacks on corporations, states, or individuals, that law enforcement does owe a duty to engage with all three entities proactively. Although cyber attacks may be a threat, law enforcement also deals with robberies, serial rapists, and other practical threats that require their attention and resources. Thus, the argument against the protection of cyber attack is that there are a plethora of additional practical issues that must be addressed first.

Overall, there is a need for prioritization. Law enforcement operates on a cost–benefit analysis in determining how to respond to various crimes. Thus, with cyber being a key issue, it results in a deflection of attention and money from real and immediate threats. Ultimately, as many would argue, that would result in a minimization of protection provided to individuals from real, practical threats, in lieu of potential cyber threats.

VIGNETTE

Imagine you are walking through a park, it is late at night and there are few people around, and three individuals come up and surround you. They demand your wallet, ID, and anything else you have. They emphasize that they will do whatever it takes to get their way, thus, you ultimately comply with their demands.

At that moment, after these three individuals have run away with your wallet, ID, and anything else valuable you may have had with you, what would be your first step? At that moment you will likely call for help. Whether the police are first, or a significant other is first, you will typically end up calling the police. And the reason for that is because the police are trained to handle situations like this and can operate in such a way to protect you, potentially not from that experience but from future experiences. In addition, police may have the ability to recover the items stolen.

Imagine now, you are an employee of a corporation that has not invested in adequate cyber protection. In that instance, you are essentially walking through a park, late at night, alone. Next,

(Continued)

malware software is implemented in your company's system, and the information is being stolen. This information involves employee records, identification information, and other confidential information. Ultimately, due to the company's lack of adequate cyber protection, they metaphorically acquiesce to the thief's demands and lose your employee information.

At that moment, once these cyber attackers have run away with your employee records, identification information, and other confidential information, what is the first step? The first step should be to call for help. However, the critical issue becomes, who do you call? Are the police equipped to handle this circumstance? Has the training been adequate? Do they have the ability to recover the items stolen? If not the police, who can help in this instance? Is there any chance to recover when you are a victim of a cyber attack? These are critical questions to consider.

THE THREAT OF CYBER

Let us examine the critical question further, the question being, does law enforcement owes a duty to states, corporations, and individuals from an amorphous tangible threat called cyber? In order to answer the question, we must step back and consider whether a cyber attack truly poses a credible threat, or is that threat exaggerated? Further, has the threat been exaggerated for various reasons, be it funding for agencies or a convenient issue of the day?

There is clear evidence of significant cyber attacks on corporations, which demonstrates the real and legitimate threat that the cyber attackers pose. Is it imminent, akin to someone preparing to rob a house? There are clear threats posed by cyber hackers. The follow-up question, do they pose a physical threat in the context of physical harm? The answer to that seems to be no.

VIGNETTE

Let us take a minute and pause to review the preceding question. The question is do cyber threats pose a physical threat in the
(Continued)

context of physical harm? The easy answer, and the answer most would assume, seems to be no. Cyber, unlike traditional terrorism, does not involve individuals attempting to inflict physical pain. However, it is essential to remember that despite this understanding, it does not mean physical pain cannot be inflicted, as a result of a cyber attack.

A cyber attack is incredibly difficult to pinpoint. Often, corporations who have been penetrated do not detect the penetration for weeks at a time. In addition, a cyber attack is extremely difficult to combat against, and often cyber protection is inadequate. Thus, these sentiments of fear of an attack, resulting in apparent weakness, or inability to halt a penetration, despite taking proactive measures, are similar sentiments to a physical attack.

Thus, many would argue that cyber attacks do not play a physical role and are not analogous to a physical threat in the context of physical harm; it can be argued that the distinction is futile. Both events, either a physical invasion of one's home or a cyber invasion of one's personal computer, violate the individual's privacy. Both events result in feelings of violation and vulnerability, and both should be categorized in a similar manner.

But, this is a critical distinction; the potential for significant economic loss as a result of cyber attackers cannot be minimized. The vulnerability of the individual to hacking their private medical records, as discussed in Chapter 6, exist as real and legitimate threats. A possible attack on government infrastructure constitutes an attack. Do they pose an immediate physical threat? Likely no. However, does that mean the threat of attack should be minimized? Absolutely not.

A successful cyber attack has the potential to cause significant damage to a variety of sources: a city's water system, airports, and air traffic control, or to electronic grids. All of these potentially cause massive economic harm. This threat cannot be minimized. The question further becomes, is it the law enforcement's responsibility to proactively engage the cyber threat? Given the sophistication of cyber attackers, our present protection mechanisms in place are potentially insufficient to minimize the threat.

To dismiss the threat of cyber is unrealistic. A proposed recommendation for law enforcement to proactively engage is critical. However, it is even more critical to find a middle ground. The middle ground requires the following. It requires three potential victims—states, corporations, and individuals—to engage with law enforcement in a conversation. This conversation is complex but will force law enforcement to prioritize threats and vulnerabilities, including cyber as one of those threats.

VIGNETTE

Listed above are three potential victims: states, corporations, and individuals. Each has the ability to store and access critical information that is likely to be penetrated in a cyber attack. Does each victim have an obligation to report to law enforcement? Does law enforcement owe each victim a duty of care, a requirement to respond and react to a cyber attack in a certain manner? Further, does the law enforcement response vary depending on the victim—specifically, whether it states corporations and individuals? We will use scenarios to help us to work through these questions.

Not only is there a need for prioritization, but also there is a cost-benefit analysis conversation about the best way to arguably use the limited resources in terms of education. The education involves dealing with government, corporations, and individuals and working with law enforcement to proactively be aware of cyber threats.

The first thing to consider, in understanding the three separate groups of victims, is whether each group has a heightened obligation to report to law enforcement as opposed to another group. Does the state, or the government, have a heightened obligation to work with law enforcement? This argument consists of the state's obligation to protect its citizens as its own. Thus, does that additional requirement of protection require it to report sooner, compared to corporations or individuals?

Consider the following victim, the corporation. Do they have a heightened responsibility to report to law enforcement? This heightened responsibility would stem for the individual's willingness to store information with a corporation. A corporation, unlike the state, does not exist as a whole to serve individuals. Rather, a corporation is typically incorporated with minimum liability and a purpose to make money.

(Continued)

However, with that understanding, a corporation also recognizes that individuals that do business with it choose to do so. And, with that choice, it is the corporation's obligation to protect their customers. Thus, do they, like the state, have a heightened obligation, as a victim, to report sooner to law enforcement? Consider the alternative. Does law enforcement have a lesser obligation to a corporation—since its primary objective is not to protect its consumer? Does law enforcement have a higher obligation to a state for the same reason—since its primary objective is to serve its citizens?

Finally, let us consider the third victim, the individual. The recommendation for law enforcement to proactively engage encompasses the most variance when dealing with individuals. Unlike corporations or states, individuals are not relegated to follow a specific code. In addition, individuals typically do not have certain parameters or requirements they must meet in order to continue being individuals. Rather, individuals make specific decisions that may, for better or worse, affect their cybersecurity.

Thus, the overall question becomes, even when finding a middle ground with each of the potential victims, is there an approach that can be applied to each, despite their drastic differences? In addition, does the obligation from law enforcement vary depending on the entity? And if it does, is that proper? Or should law enforcement apply equally to each entity, regardless of the parameters or benchmarks the entity abides by? These difficult questions continue to be unanswered today.

The critical points to move forward in the discussion with law enforcement are given in Figure 8.1.

To establish the above points, it is imperative that law enforcement proactively educates. Law enforcement officials must train themselves in the realm of cyber to better understand the risks posed by such.

- Prioritize our resources
- Have a cost-benefit discussion about effective training of the public
- Articulate and define what is effective and what is ineffective in regard to training

Figure 8.1 Law enforcement points.

LAW ENFORCEMENT EDUCATION

Below is a discussion I had recently with a senior law enforcement official tasked with tracking sophisticated money laundering through cyber. This official was extremely well intentioned, in that he understood how important it was for him to be engaged in the tracking of laundering for the purpose of combating the drug industry. However, he also made the point that he had multiple other obligations. These other obligations consisted of the points listed in Figure 8.2. Thus, he did not have the resources to engage in the type of tracking necessary to minimize the threat posed by cyber.

Although this official's intentions were nothing but the best, the frustration was palpable and predicated on the following. There are several reasons that make law enforcement struggle in dealing with the realities of cyber protection, which are given in Figure 8.3.

Overall, a proactive education in training is essential. In addition, there is a need for law enforcement agencies to cooperate with one another. This cooperation must occur on local, state, and national levels. Law enforcement must engage in a sophisticated cooperation plan to more adequately respond to the threat posed.

The necessity of cooperation

My background, specifically my work in operational counterterrorism, demonstrated the necessity of that cooperation. However, that cooperation is not always a reality. The reality is cooperation is difficult.

- Dealing with criminals presently engaged in the committing of crime
- Cooperating with banks
- Creating cooperation methods with other financial institutions
- Educating the public on potential threats

Figure 8.2 Law enforcement obligations.

- Insufficient training and education to engage in sophisticated tracking
- Chain of command, coinciding with a lack of access and prioritization to the real and apparent threat of cyber
- Lack of cooperation among distinct law enforcement agencies
- Lack of cooperation among the community

Figure 8.3 Law enforcement realities.

1. Institutionalize cooperation between peer law enforcement agencies
2. Institutionalize bottom-up and top-down cooperation, meaning state to federal and federal to state
3. Effective training of law enforcement in dealing with cyber threats

Figure 8.4 Cooperation steps.

The steps to be taken for cooperation are given in Figure 8.4.

Let us consider the following example. A number of years ago, I had a lunch meeting with state, local, and federal agencies. The point of the meeting was to have a conversation about information sharing. The body language in this room was clear. The federal agencies are going to be extremely hesitant to share sensitive information with local agencies. This model of hesitation suggests something that potentially, there is a sense of institutional jealousy. The lack of cooperation with respect to intelligence sharing will guarantee that cyber hackers will consistently have the upper hand, because they benefit from the lack of cooperation.

Educating the public is absolutely essential. Education of the public will further the cooperation among local, state, and federal agencies. Without it, it would be impossible to put together the type of sophisticated counter attack model that is required to minimize the threat posed by cyber. However, it is incorrect to argue that this cooperation model guarantees that there will be no more cyber attacks.

That is a fallacy. But to minimize the threat and vulnerabilities of cyber attack, this cooperation is essential. I formerly testified in Congress on a similar issue, involving a cooperation-based model a number of years ago. In this testimony, I furthered the argument that

VIGNETTE

As discussed above, there must be an emphasis on intelligence sharing among local, state, and federal agencies. Without such sharing and cooperation, cyber hackers will consistently outsmart and thwart cyber protection, specifically because those attempting to prevent against it will lack the requisite skills and expertise. Consider the following analogy to help depict the flaws that come as a result of a lack of cooperation.

(Continued)

Imagine an elementary school. In order for an elementary school to be successful, for each student to get the quality of education they require, several layers are involved. The bottom layer, the one that works closest with the students, is the teacher. This layer's responsibility is to monitor for classroom struggles, or moments of penetration for a cyber attacker. If one specific individual is struggling to grasp a concept, their job is to ensure they reach a level equivalent to that of their peers. In addition, extra steps might be required to notify those higher up of the student.

This is similar to a point of penetration for a cyber attacker. In addition, the organization or corporation is like the teacher. It is their job to monitor their company and ensure the points of penetration, the students struggling to grasp a concept, have additional attention. Also, it is their obligation to report the points of penetration to a higher up, meaning local, state, or federal agencies, or law enforcement. Without the corporation's diligence and reporting, the agencies or law enforcement would have no way of knowing of that specific point of penetration. In addition, without a teacher recommending additional help for a specific student, it would be very difficult for a principal to realize who needs additional help.

Beyond the teacher, you have the school's administration system, specifically the principal and vice principal. These roles are equivalent to agencies, both at the local, state, and federal levels. The administration, the principal, and the vice principal have a duty to monitor the school, ensure the best care for the students, and maintain a safe environment.

Similarly, agencies have an obligation to corporations that exist within it, at the local, state, and federal levels, to do the same. They must monitor the corporations or organizations, ensure they are acting in the best manner, and maintain a cooperative sphere that they can operate their business within. If a teacher is not reporting to the administration, they are unable to serve as effectively as they could. In addition, if the administration is not willing to support the teacher when needs are recognized, the teacher will be less likely to cooperate or rely on the administration's services.

(Continued)

This is similar with cyber attacks. If a corporation or organization reports points of penetration to the local, state, and federal agencies, they do so with the understanding that those agencies will cooperate and assist to protect against cyber attackers. In addition, the agencies rely on the corporations or organizations to report those penetration points, so they can best meet their needs.

The final level to consider is the guidance counselor at the elementary school. The guidance counselor role incorporates many duties. Specifically, a guidance counselor is meant to assist the teachers in their ability to ensure the highest quality of care for students. In addition, the guidance counselor assists the administration, specifically the principal and vice principal, in making sure that the actions they are taking are appropriate and effective. The guidance counselor serves as a bridge between the two, with the ultimate goal of developing the most effective means to serve the children.

Law enforcement performs the role of the guidance counselor. Specifically, law enforcement is meant to be that bridge between corporations and organizations and local, state, and federal agencies, and helping all to develop the most effective ways to fight against cyber attackers. Law enforcement assists corporations in their ability to thwart future attacks by developing training to recognize points of penetration common among corporations and developing ways to fight against it. In addition, law enforcement helps agencies in making sure that they are responding specifically to the needs from corporations and spending time and money on what really counts.

Overall, each role in an elementary school plays a pivotal role. The teacher, at the closest level to the individual, plays the role of recognizing needs and responding to them. Similarly, the corporation or organization at the closest level to the points of penetration plays the role of filling in holes as it spots them.

The administration, or the local, state, and federal agencies, plays the crucial role of supporting the teachers in their prevention against points of penetration. Their job is to cooperate and assist as best they can, playing off the expertise of the teachers,

(Continued)

or corporations. Finally, the guidance counselor bridges the gap. Specifically, the counselor helps to develop and implement the most effective mechanism to serve the children. Similarly, law enforcement develops the requisite training and mechanism to best thwart future cyber attacks. In addition, law enforcement creates documentation of past cyber attacks, in the hope of recognizing previous points of penetration and preventing future similarities among corporations and organizations.

without cooperation among the distinct agencies, it will be impossible to develop a sophisticated counterterrorism.

This level of sophistication only occurs if there is that well-rounded cooperation among local, state, and federal levels. In talking about both cooperation and education, the third point is training.

It is essential that law enforcement trains itself with respect to cybersecurity, the threats posed by it, and the measures that most effectively enable responding to cybersecurity. To engage in such training, it requires law enforcement to think outside the box. This requires all of us, public and law enforcement, to put on our creative hats and think as cyber attackers are potentially thinking.

TRAINING OF LAW ENFORCEMENT

Law enforcement must proactively engage in sophisticated, consistent, and institutionalized cooperation with agencies around the world. The individual executing a cyber attack is sitting somewhere in the world posing a threat, not only to the United States but also outside the United States. Thus, the kind of cooperation must extend outside our nation. It would be a fallacy to say this does or does not already occur.

This cooperation does not occur to the extent it needs to because the kinds of threats that must be protected against are international in scope. Think back to the former law enforcement officials who dealt with the money laundering. For those officials to more effectively engage in responding and minimizing the threat posed, they needed to extend outside the United States in scope, since it is clearly an international issue.

Sticking with the law enforcement official who dealt with money laundering, not only was that individual denied cooperation from the agencies above him, in terms of federal and state levels, he also did not have full cooperation internationally. In order for that individual to effectively minimize the threat, it requires international officials to cooperate with each other, train with each other, and educate each other. Overall, cyber poses such a threat that if we do not engage in this three-part cooperation, local, state, and federal, as well as training and education, then law enforcement will be significantly handicapped.

VIGNETTE

Consider for a minute, you receive a letter in the mail stating you are delinquent on several credit cards, and you must pay in 90 days. The first thing to consider is, what are these credit cards? For the sake of the example, assume all credit cards were opened without your knowledge due to a cyber breach which resulted in your social security number being stolen. You are now a victim of identity theft. But, who do you report to when you are a victim of identity theft? You can call the local police. However, what if the theft happened in Florida? This makes it a cross jurisdictional issue. Does the diversity of jurisdiction turn this issue into a federal issue?

Overall, is the breach that resulted in identity theft one that is being handled. In addition, if it is being handled by one law enforcement agency, is there necessary reporting between agencies to best ameliorate the problem? In addition, has the agency had adequate training on how to respond to cyber threat? Has the agency had adequate training on how to potentially remedy a cyber threat? Without such training, turning to law enforcement in the event of a cyber attack would seem useless.

IMPORTANCE OF LAW ENFORCEMENT WITH CYBER

As said in the beginning, we have taught our children, and encouraged law enforcement to teach our children, not to get in cars with strangers. Why? Because we know that when some children have gone in cars with strangers, unimaginable horrors have befallen those children. Just as we have trained our children not to get in cars with strangers, it is necessary to train individuals to keep their private information safe. When we are online, if someone requests your social security information, do not give it to them. This responsibility of education begins with law enforcement training the public.

This responsibility goes both ways: law enforcement must educate, and corporations must come forward with instances of a cyber attack. In Chapter 7, the discussion revolved around corporations. In it, we discussed the responsibility of corporations to come forward and notify law enforcement once hacked. A corporation must come forward to law enforcement to identify where they are vulnerable and what measures can be taken to minimize the threat moving forward. Without this step, without corporations coming forward and sharing that information, there is no way that law enforcement can effectively begin the process of creating effective counter cybersecurity measures. Thus, the burden rests on corporations to step up and come forward.

EXAMPLE OF CORPORATIONS

Let us consider an example. Let us say that Corporation X has been hacked. Once hacked, Corporation X comes to the local police chief, or state department, or the U.S. Department of Homeland Security and reports the incident. For that conversation to be effective, it will require that law enforcement have the sufficient skills to address the incident. In addressing the incident, the law enforcement will need to work with Corporation X's IT team to understand where the attack occurred, the various points of vulnerability, and the best steps to minimize the threat.

Corporations are hesitant to come forward, because it will impact their economic model, shareholders' perception, and consumer perception. However, a corporation putting their proverbial *head in the sand* is not a solution. Corporations have an obligation to report to law enforcement. There is proposed legislation that imposes on corporations the obligation to report a hack, and that is a step in the right direction. Corporations cannot fear the threat of economic impact or shareholder disappointment. The long-term impact of not reporting, not understanding the points of vulnerability, and not understanding how to minimize future threats far outweighs the short-term economic or shareholder disappointment.

However, for this conversation to even be possible, law enforcement must have the skills, training, and resources. There are points of vulnerability in corporations, and law enforcement must understand the corporation before they can understand those points. In order to determine the points, law enforcement must work with the corporation's IT team to determine those points. This is the only way that the law enforcement can effectively minimize the threat moving forward.

Back to our example, once Corporation X comes to law enforcement, law enforcement can begin to recognize a pattern of the cyber attacks. Law enforcement can recognize, not only a pattern against Corporation X, but possibly a pattern in a similar size corporation in a different location that was attacked in a similar way. This begins the process of creating a pattern. In developing such a pattern, it can be determined whether the attack was caused by the same hacker. The only way that will happen is when Corporation X informs its local law enforcement. Thus, the cooperation model is between corporation and law enforcement, as well as law enforcement to corporation.

CONCLUSION

Overall, a cyber attack is a form of unconventional terrorism that absolutely requires unconventional measures, which requires the need for cooperation. The second point is a requirement for training. The third point rests on a responsibility to train and educate. Thus, this is a three-fold approach: cooperation, training, and education. It is fully recognizable that this approach is not cheap. It is a drain on existing resources and requires a discussion about reprioritizing resources.

If indeed cyber threats pose the dangers suggested, it is a requirement to consider how vulnerable we are to cyber attacks in order to have a more sophisticated and creative model in play. Overall, law enforcement needs to come to corporations, state leaders, and individuals, and offer a hand. It requires law enforcement to rearticulate its existing model of law enforcement.

The questions to be considered in reviewing Chapter 8 are given in Figure 8.5.

- Does law enforcement have an obligation to educate the public?
- Does law enforcement have an obligation to spend significant resources on cybersecurity?
- What is law enforcement's obligation to cooperate with other law enforcement agencies?
- What is the obligation of federal, state, and local law enforcement agencies to cooperate with one another?
- What is the obligation of law enforcement to notify the public of cyber attacks or potential cyber attacks?

Figure 8.5 Review questions.

9 Cybersecurity in the future

INTRODUCTION

This chapter emphasizes cybersecurity in the future, the enormity of the risk, and the steps to be taken to mitigate that risk. The use of various scenarios will make the conversation more realistic and less theoretical. This is done to help the reader understand cybersecurity on its most practical level.

SCENARIO A

Individual A receives a phone call. On the other end of the line, someone is claiming to be from an agency asking you to provide confirmation of identity, address, or last name. This individual on the other line claims to be from a credit card agency or financial institution that needs to do a background check on you.

Last year, I received a call from someone at the Internal Revenue Service (IRS) claiming I had back taxes owed. This individual threatened that if I did not pay these back taxes by a certain date, I would run afoul of the law. In order to pay those back taxes, the individual requested my credit card information. I understood that call was a scam and quickly hung up the phone. But, that may not be another individual's first reaction. Some people may jump to the conclusion and assume they have done something wrong.

Typically, once the individual steps back from the situation, they can recognize it as a scam. However, not everyone can have that foresight. The statistics clearly demonstrate that an extraordinary number of Americans fall victim to scams like the scenario above. In addressing those situations, it costs a tremendous amount of money.

This means the hackers are not only successful, they are also taxing an extreme cost on our society. The cyber attackers are able to hack into our systems, receive telephone numbers, and tax a great cost on our society.

Let us take a step back to Scenario A. The first thing the individual should do is cut off the call. Or even take a step further, and do not answer the call. But if you do answer, do not give your social security number or any information, and just simply end the call.

SCENARIO B

Individual B receives a phone call. The person calling claims they are from the police department. This person says if Individual B does not pay a certain amount, they will be arrested or their home will be searched. The first thing that must be done once the call is finished is you alert the local law enforcement agency that the cyber attacker purported to be. It is critical that you report the conversation that was a scam.

In addition, if the phone number being used is the actual number of the police department, not only is the name being used, but their system has been hacked. Thus, it is an absolute must that you notify the relevant police department. Then, the responsibility falls to the law enforcement. The question arises, what should the law enforcement do with that information?

It is essential for law enforcement to do the following. First, create a mechanism whereby they can inform the public. This information can come through radio stations, television stations, posts on their home page, or other ways. Second, inform other agencies that their number has been hacked. Third, inform the FBI that their number has been hacked.

This effort goes back to Chapter 7, involving prioritization of resources and a cost–benefit analysis. In regards to Scenario B, with the police officer scam, let us take a step farther in the steps that should be taken. Imagine, after you have received a call, you report it to the local agency. You call the dispatcher, and the dispatcher's simple response is, "thank you very much, we're aware of the situation, thank you." That is an insufficient response.

The more correct response would have been for the dispatcher to get as much information as possible from the individual in attempts to create a composite of the types of calls being conducted, the information being asked so that they can create a profile. In actively profiling the hacker, law enforcement is taking those essential first steps to address the situation.

Let us take a step back to Scenario A. Individual A received the phone call from the IRS. The initial assumption or reaction, being that they have done something wrong, is incorrect. It is essential to have a transformation of thinking from the fear of doing something wrong to the assumption that the caller is nefarious, one who is violating Individual A to gather information. The individual's response should be much more aggressive. The response should be immediate, to cut off the call, notify law enforcement, and trust them to proactively engage with other law enforcement.

SCENARIO C

This next scenario will address the different groups affected by cyber, including corporations and government. For this scenario, consider an airline has been hacked. The possible ramifications of a hack of an aircraft, or air control tower, are enormous. This is a similar scenario found in a popular movie with Bruce Willis, *Live Free or Die Hard*. If an airline has been hacked, there is a way to manipulate the airline, plane, or air control system. With that hack, there are two different groupings that are negatively impacted.

The first impacted group is the corporation, specifically the airline. The second impacted group is the government, specifically the Federal Aviation Association and the air traffic control tower. Thus, this analysis requires discussion from a variety of perspectives. In such analysis, the emphasis comes back to cooperation. It is essential that the two impacted groups, the airline and the government, cooperate.

Thus, we step back to reactions that should exist after each scenario. First, there must be immediate notification of the hack. But, as mentioned in previous chapters, there is a great disparity between the corporations who report an attack versus those who have actually been attacked. If an airline fears it has been a victim of a cyber attack, even though there may be a negative repercussion or consumer trepidation, the reality is those concerns are minimal in comparison to the requirement of protecting those in the air and report the attack.

In order for airlines to effectively report, it is essential to institutionalize efficient reporting mechanisms between an airline and the air control tower. In addition to a connection between airlines and the air control tower, there must be a connection among other airlines, including competitors. For us to minimize the negative impact posed by hackers, there is a need for corporations to cooperate with one another, despite the threat of competition. Overall, the number one priority must be passenger safety, not fear of economic reprisal or shareholder disappointment.

Take, for example, someone who flies a great deal, even weekly. This individual is well acquainted with the airline, as well as the passenger safety instruction given at the beginning of each flight. In that instruction, the airline emphasizes passenger safety, making it the airline's number one priority. Thus, if the airline felt or was concerned about being hacked, the absolute requirement is a double reporting mechanism, one to the government and one to other airlines.

The question becomes, what should the government, meaning the Federal Aviation Administration or Department of Homeland Security, do? As a concerned flier, I suggest creating a checklist in terms of responding to and minimizing the threat. First, if an airplane has been hacked and a plane is in the air, relevant contingency plans must be applied. The threat of manipulating planes in the air exists as a terrorist attack. This attack can result in the loss of life in the exact same way as a conventional terrorist attack.

Being that a cyber attack has the equivalent threat level of a conventional terrorist attack, there must be a contingency plan, in this scenario, for landing a plane in an emergency. Although this may be a passenger inconvenience, and a cost imposition, it is incumbent upon government agencies involved in the airline industry to create a contingency plan. It requires an intensive program to identify how the airline was attacked. This goes back to the conversation of points of vulnerability.

POINTS OF VULNERABILITY

All industries have points of vulnerability. An airline suffering a cyber hack requires the airline to consider those points of vulnerability and identify where the hack occurred. This must be done quickly because the airlines need to keep flying. Millions of Americans everyday need to fly; thus, the airlines must keep functioning.

However, an intelligent response to a cyber attack against an airline is to halt the flights in order to engage and determine where the hack occurred. The airline must establish sophisticated cyber counterresponses, and the best way to do so is by implementing a point of vulnerability analysis. Overall, we cannot view a cyber attack against an airline as something that is here today and gone tomorrow; it will not work like that.

Responses to this type of situation require cooperation between corporations and the government. It requires the government to impose limits on corporations, which are potentially *no-fly* periods. It may require the government to impose on the airline additional costs about creating an enhanced, sophisticated firewall. Creating these firewalls takes time. However, in walking through those points of vulnerability, the need for firewalls becomes more apparent.

MOVING FORWARD

In this critical conversation of cybersecurity in the future, the threat is significant. The threat by hackers on both the individual and corporation level must be viewed akin to an act of war. If the attack comes from a nonstate actor, then it technically is not an act of war, seeing that nonstate actors cannot declare war on states. However, it is a significant act of aggression. This act of aggression requires the nation-state, the corporation, and the individual to understand that cyber threats and cyber attacks are real and significant.

In that context, the cyber attack may have the possibility to harm us. The following kinds of attacks on infrastructure may have the possibility to harm us. Take for instance, an attack on the following: a city's water system, a city's transportation system, a hospital system, and an airline computer system.

The above are examples of cyber attacks that go far beyond your credit card being hacked. The above scenarios demonstrate the points given in Figure 9.1.

For those reasons, it is imperative that we consider cyber attacks as a threat that merits serious reflection.

Thus, the question becomes, what can we, as an individual, do to better protect ourselves? Or, even to better protect corporations, cities, states, or the country from cyber attackers? A cyber attack is potentially dangerous and an extremely volatile attack with enormous

---

- Instill great fear
- Intimidate the civilian population
- Potentially harm individuals
- Potentially result in deaths

Figure 9.1 Effects of a hack.

consequences and ramifications. Those ramifications reflect the true intent of nefarious cyber hacks that goes well beyond a credit card scam. This threat necessitates the need to educate the public, train our individuals, and more effectively cooperate on a local, state, and federal level to address this critical issue.

FURTHER DISCUSSION POINTS

In previous chapters, many cybersecurity concerns regarding geopolitics and international law were discussed, including the intricacies that occur in dealing with cyber on a global scale. Developing a cybersecurity policy was discussed thoroughly in Chapter 4, specifically with the ramifications of implementing such a policy.

The initial chapters focused on reactions, how corporations respond to cybercrime, and possibly how they should respond to cybercrime. Following that discussion, the next chapters emphasize how individuals can mitigate the effects of cybersecurity, and potentially how law enforcement ought to mitigate cybersecurity. Chapter 8 emphasizes various scenarios meant to address the threat of cybersecurity in the future.

This chapter continues the discussion, walking through various cybersecurity scenarios and detailing the steps that likely are taken, steps that potentially should be taken, and steps that should be avoided. Each scenario will be one that you, as the reader, can likely relate either through personal experience or watching it happen to a company or individuals around you.

The overall message to accept is that the world of cybersecurity is broad and touches all corners of our lives. The sooner we, as individuals, prepare and protect against cyber attacks, the sooner corporations, law enforcement, and government agencies are likely to do the same.

SCENARIO D

Imagine you are sitting at home, enjoying your favorite television show, and the phone rings, a call from a number you do not recognize. Many of us, if we do not recognize the phone number, do not answer the call. We quickly Google the number and determine that it is from a collection agency, and the purpose of their call is to alert you of outstanding accounts under your name. This is often the first sign of one's identity being stolen.

It is easy to deduce the collection calls were not for you, if the accounts in question are under a different name than yours, although one very similar (e.g., Ms. Right Investments versus Ms. Wright Investments). In addition, if these accounts exist in Florida, and you have never been to Florida, that is another trigger of your identity being stolen.

Another trigger in considering whether your identity has been stolen is determining whether an unauthorized individual had access to your secure information. One way this occurs is by leaving your social security card out in the public. However, this is unlikely because the majority of us have more common sense. One likely way an unauthorized individual can access your secure information is through a data breach. As mentioned in Chapter 2, the breach at Target impacted 70 million individuals. This likely affected credit card information.

Breaches at insurance agencies and schools can affect one's social security number. Consider, when applying to a school, in the application it is likely you included your social security number and home address. Thus, if an educational institution is vulnerable to a cyber attack and is breached, your social security number can be accessed. This is often the path taken for identity theft.

Thus, at this point, you have a very difficult situation to handle. It is a situation that will not go away by ignoring it and requires some type of action. The next steps in the scenario will be considering the various paths you can take in dealing with the situation (Figure 9.2).

Having your identity stolen is a significant ordeal. It affects many aspects of your life, including several you may not have considered initially. It affects your ability to open a bank account, take out a loan, buy a house, or open a new business. Basically, having your identity stolen puts a scarlet A on your social security number. Thus, the question then becomes, what is there for compensation?

In asking one individual who was a victim of identity theft whether they were compensated after their identity was stolen, they vehemently emphasized that they were not compensated. In addition, it took them several years to figure out the magnitude of the effect that occurred from their identity being stolen. Those additional implications consisted of another individual filing taxes for them, and thus collecting their income tax return. Their suggestion for compensation is that it should come from the federal government. Or, if no compensation can be offered, there should at least be a measure to change one's social security number.

Path A: Do nothing. Hope the collection agencies forget about it, or someone else pays the outstanding bills, and continue to ignore the calls.

Path B: Call the collection agency and fight back, claiming the outstanding accounts are not your problem. Threaten law enforcement and ultimately realize the account is under your social security number and tied to your credit. Then, do nothing.

Path C: Research various methods, determine the best response, and act accordingly. This may include reporting a misused social security number, closing all new accounts in your name, or correcting your credit report. It should always include reporting identity theft to the Federal Trade Commission.

Path D: Minimize the impact. In addition to the steps in Plan C, further the minimization of the impact by filing with Equifax (or a similarly related company) and take any additional steps as instructed by the Federal Trade Commission.

Figure 9.2 Potential paths.

As seen with credit cards, if that information is breached, the credit card company issues you a new card. Thus, the question can be asked, can the federal government issue new social security numbers when one's identity is stolen? It is an important question to consider. Overall, there are several paths one can take in reacting to their social security number being breached, meaning their identity is stolen, and the path chosen significantly affects the ramifications felt by the breach.

SCENARIO E

Although the individual scenario detailed above may resonate with more individuals, the corporate scenario discussed next is one with the potential for a more catastrophic impact. First, in presenting this scenario, it is essential to consider four different corporations, each with a distinct difference. Corporation A is one of the largest corporations in America.

From that, Corporation A assumes great responsibility in the amount of information it accesses. Therefore, Corporation A invested significant money and time in cyber protection. It works closely with law enforcement, engages in employee trainings, and actively employs several data experts to protect their corporation against a cyber attack.

Now, despite all their best efforts, Corporation A has been breached. Similar to Target or eBay, over 100 million customers have now been affected by the breach. The question then becomes, what is the next step, and who has a responsibility in the aftermath of the attack? As seen with previous examples, the U.S. government has taken it upon themselves to get involved when corporations exist of a certain size. But the question becomes, since Corporation A took significant measures to protect themselves from a cyber attack, and fell victim anyway, should the compensation or retaliation be greater since they took steps to try to prevent the event?

Either way, the first thing that must occur when a company is the victim of a cyber attack is notification to law enforcement. Although companies may not want to report, for fear of customer doubt or repercussion, this need be a legal obligation. Without notification to law enforcement, law enforcement is unable to create patterns or algorithms that could prevent future attacks.

The next thing to consider is whether Corporation A has absolved liability, because they took the necessary precautions and, through no fault of their own, still fell prey to a cyber attack. This is difficult to answer and one that may not fully answered until additional legislation is put into place.

Now we will consider Corporation B. Corporation B, like Corporation A, is one of the largest corporations in America. From that, Corporation B assumes great responsibility in the amount of information it accesses. However, Corporation B has not invested significant money or time in cyber protection. Rather, their board of directors, who is actively aware of the threat of cybersecurity, voted to delay any financial or personnel investment in the pursuit of cyber protection because that is expensive, and the corporation is in the business of making money. This issue is the pinnacle of the protection versus profit debate.

Now, imagine Corporation B has been breached. Similar to Target or eBay, over 100 million customers have now been affected by the breach. The question then becomes, what is the next step, and who has a responsibility in the aftermath of the attack? As mentioned earlier, the U.S. government may take it upon themselves to get involved when corporations exist of a certain size, as they have done previously.

But the question becomes, since Corporation B did not take significant measures to protect themselves from a cyber attack, and fell victim, should the compensation or retaliation be less since they did not take steps to prevent the event? As mentioned before, either way, the first thing that needs to occur when a company is the victim of a cyber attack is notification of such attack to law enforcement. Usually, most companies do not want to report, whether it is fear of customer doubt or shareholder perception, or other repercussion, it needs to be a legal obligation. The next thing to consider is whether Corporation B is increasingly liable for its negligence.

Unlike Corporation A, their liability cannot be absolved in any way because they did not take necessary precautions. Despite likely recommendations from the chief intelligence officer (CIO), or other employees in the corporation, Corporation B chose profit over protection and became an easy target. The question then becomes, due to their negligence, should the compensation or protection postattack be less? That is a question that will need to be determined by future legislation.

Now we will consider Corporation C. Corporation C, unlike Corporations A and B, is one of the smaller corporations in America, a small-town business held closely by a few family members. From that, Corporation C assumes significantly less responsibility in the amount of information it accesses.

However, like Corporation A, Corporation C has invested significant money and time in cyber protection. They work closely with law enforcement, engage in employee training, and actively employ a data expert to protect their corporation against a cyber attack.

Despite Corporation C's best efforts, they have been breached. However, unlike Corporations A and B, the breach does not affect over 100 million customers. Rather, the breach affects simply 5000 individuals. The question still becomes, what is the next step, and who has a responsibility in the aftermath of the attack? It is safe to assume that the U.S. government is less likely to get involved when the breach is so minimal, as compared to Corporations A and B.

However, the question to be asked is, since Corporation C took significant measures to protect themselves from a cyber attack, and fell victim anyway, should they be compensated or supported in some way more than a company that made no effort to protect against a cyber attack?

Corporation C, despite its small size in comparison to Corporations A and B, must still have a legal obligation to report to law enforcement as the victim of a cyber attack. After which the next question to consider is whether Corporation C absolves liability, because they took the necessary precaution and, through no fault of their own, still fell prey to a cyber attack.

The final corporation is Corporation D. Corporation D, unlike Corporations A and B, but similar to Corporation C, is one of the smaller corporations in America, a small-town business held closely by a few family members. From that, Corporation D assumes significantly less responsibility in the amount of information it accesses. However, like Corporation B, Corporation D has not invested significant money or time in cyber protection.

Rather, the corporation decided to delay any financial or personnel investment in the pursuit of cyber protection because it is expensive, and the corporation is focused on making money. This issue, as demonstrated with Corporation B as well, is the pinnacle of the protection versus profit debate.

Due to Corporation D's lack of effort, they have been breached. However, unlike Corporations A and B, the breach does not affect over 100 million customers. Rather, the breach affects simply 5000 individuals. The reasoning and considerations now become very similar to the questions that occurred with the breach in Corporation C. The question still becomes, what is the next step, and who has a responsibility in the aftermath of the attack?

It is safe to assume that the U.S. government is less likely to get involved when the breach is so minimal, as compared to Corporations A and B. But the question becomes, since Corporation D did not take significant measures to protect themselves from a cyber attack, and fell victim, should the compensation or retaliation be less since they did not take steps to prevent the event?

Corporation D, despite its small size in comparison to Corporations A and B, must still have a legal obligation to report as the victim of a cyber attack. The next question to consider is liability. Unlike Corporations A and C, their liability cannot be absolved in any way, because they did not take necessary precautions.

Despite likely recommendations from the CIO, or other employees in the corporation, Corporation D chose profit over protection and became an easy target. The question then becomes, due to their negligence, should the compensation or protection postattack be less? That is a question that will need to be determined by future legislation.

Overall, there are many factors that come into play when a corporation is breached. The requirement to implement adequate cybersecurity protection is an issue that is currently being debated. It begs the question, should a corporation of a certain size, with access to certain records, be required to implement a certain level of cybersecurity protection in exchange for access to the critical information?

In addition, the requirement, or potential requirement, to notify law enforcement is an ongoing issue. Should a breach of a certain size have a strict liability requirement that forces companies to report the breach immediately?

Another difficulty to discover is the language barrier. This language barrier is not one you usually think of when you hear the phrase *language barrier*. It does not involve one individual speaking Spanish and another speaking French.

Rather, this language barrier occurs between individuals from different departments with radically different goals. Individuals from the IT department speak the language of tech operations and protection—and that is their sole focus. Individuals from the financial department speak the language of profits and real costs— and that is their sole focus. Thus, it is critical in any corporation to have employees or individuals that can speak both languages, stress the importance of each goal, and find a way to make both accessible (Figures 9.3 and 9.4).

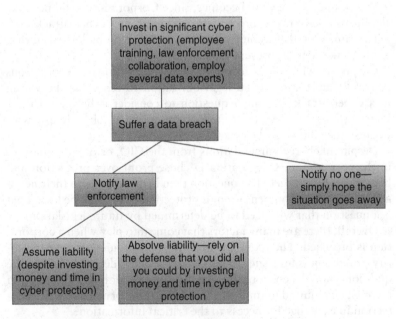

Figure 9.3 Data breach in a corporation with significant protection.

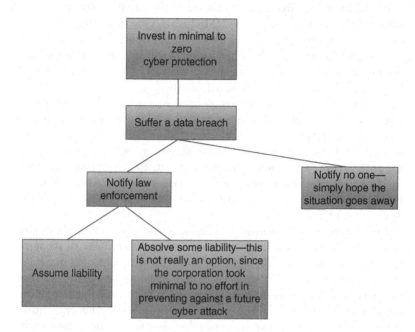

Figure 9.4 Data breach in a corporation without significant protection.

CYBER ATTACKS USED FOR GOOD

One final thing to consider is the instances where cyber activity can be used to achieve an end goal that is not malicious or bad, rather, to attempt to achieve a goal that many would find desirable. For instance, Anonymous, which is a group of loosely affiliated hackers who attempt to achieve an end goal through cyber means, has promoted several such instances.

These hackers are incredibly well versed in the realm of cybersecurity and have the power to use that skill either for good or bad. Anonymous is sometimes looked down upon, because they are trying to breach state secrets or frustrate a particular corporation's cybersecurity team. However, other times they land on the good side, a side that many can rally behind.

In recent months, Anonymous has declared war on the Islamic State of Iraq and Syria (ISIS). In a video published after the terrorist attacks in Paris in November, Anonymous declared that these "terrorist attacks cannot be left unpunished." Specifically, Anonymous stated that there would be *numerous cyber attacks* and *war has been triggered*.

In addition, Anonymous threatened action against those responsible for the water crisis in Flint, Michigan. One day after the threat of action by Anonymous, the Hurley Medical Center confirmed it was the victim of a cyber attack. The Hurley Medical Center employed the doctor who initially raised flags of concern regarding elevated lead levels in children living in Flint, Michigan.

In addition, the Michigan.gov website was attacked the following day, two days after Anonymous posted a video threatening action against those responsible for the water crisis. Due to its timely nature, it is simple to jump to the conclusion that Anonymous was responsible for both events. With the water crisis in Flint, and the terrorist attacks in Paris, and the declaration of war against ISIS by Anonymous, it introduces a different conversation and emphasis behind the notion of cybersecurity.

These examples demonstrate instances where cyber methods are used as a catalyst for a sense of good, as a way to either call recognition to an injustice or fight against those who are promoting injustice. Either way, the critical thing to recognize is the variety of impact that cybersecurity has not only in the form of a cyber attack but also in the form of rallying individuals together and promoting a general cause. As we move forward to an increasingly cyber world, this impact will only increase.

The questions to be considered in reviewing Chapter 9 are given in Figure 9.5.

- How great of a threat is cybersecurity?
- Is the threat of cyber attacks exaggerated?
- What duties or obligations do we as individuals have in addressing the threat?
- What is the duty owed by the government to the individual with respect to cyber?
- Is the duty owed the same with respect to each country and to each individual?

Figure 9.5 Review questions.

10 Final word

Of the many points raised in this book, there are three, in particular, I hope will be very much in the public eye. It is my hope this book will facilitate discussion regarding the following points given in Figure 10.1.

These three issues are, I believe, the crux of the legal and policy aspects of cyber; individually and collectively, they represent where the rubber *hits the road*. Until we have the requisite discussions, until national leaders and corporate officers truly confront the extraordinary threats posed by cybercrime and cyberterrorism, we, individually and collectively, will continue to be vulnerable and *at risk*.

In many ways, the three issues have a unifying theme: To whom is a duty owed and who owes that duty?

In the preceding pages, a number of issues relevant to cybersecurity have been raised with a particular focus on legal and policy questions. Although technical questions were of the utmost importance, they were not the focus. The larger question, hence the title *final word*, is where do we go from here? Perhaps, more than anything else, it is the critical point of inquiry for reader and author.

Throughout the book, a series of vignettes were incorporated to confront the reader with difficult circumstances and issues, many of which are real-life examples. The purpose of those vignettes was to highlight the complexity of the issue, facilitate greater discussion, and hopefully lead to resolution of many of the open-ended issues. In a book of this nature, vignettes are particularly important, given the range and scope of the dilemmas presented. There are, in many instances, neither perfect nor clear answers to the questions. This should not be a surprise, given the complexity of cybersecurity.

- Cooperation between law enforcement agencies
- Greater willingness of corporate leaders to directly address cyber threats
- Articulating and implementing the limits of state responsibility regarding cybercrime and cyberterrorism

---

Figure 10.1 Discussion points.

For example, an important inquiry such as "is an attack on a major corporation an attack on a nation-state?" raises powerfully compelling and conflicting responses. When I posed this question to academics, law enforcement officials, and cyber professionals, their answers varied, often at odds with each other. What is interesting to note is the majority's instinctual response was *yes*. This changed, sometimes, to a *maybe* when the question required unpacking. One conversation in particular stood out.

The individual in question is the vice president of corporate security for a major American corporation that has assets internationally. This company has been the subject of attacks over the years. The attacks are a direct result of their product. Therefore, there is a heightened sense of awareness and vulnerability among C level executives. When I asked him the question, the immediate response was "yes, of course." My assumption is the answer reflects the sobering realities of previous attacks. However, there was an interesting caveat to his response: "The 'yes' depends on the size of the corporation." I was unclear as to what he meant and requested that he expound on his answer. He graciously did so.

In his opinion, the *yes* is predicated exclusively on an attack on a *major* corporation. Attacks on mid-sized and small corporations, according to this individual, are not to be construed as warranting a response by the U.S. government. When I asked him whether a traditional terrorist attack on a mid-sized or small corporation would justify government action, his answer was an unequivocal *yes*.

I have known this person for years and have the greatest respect for his insight and professional experience in American law enforcement. The dissonance of his response between traditional terrorism and cyberterrorism was particularly helpful in my efforts to understand the differences between the two. The consequences of the former are obvious, unlike the latter. Furthermore, life and property damage make for powerful visuals that can serve to propel public and decision makers alike.

The media plays an important role in highlighting the harm caused. The attendant drama in the aftermath of a successful attack resulting in death cannot be captured, when client accounts are hacked in a cyber attack. The adage, "one picture is worth a thousand words," does not apply when a hack has occurred. This is not to minimize the impact, but it serves to explain, at least in part, the answers provided to my question. Rallying around the flag is understandable in the wake of a traditional terrorist attack; that visceral response is hard to conjure after the target has been hacked. The same applies to Sony and an endless number of other U.S. companies.

The question is whether that divided response serves national security interests. Rearticulated: What are the limits of government involvement in cybersecurity? The easy answer is that cybersecurity is a priority for local, state, and national government. The harder question is what does that mean and is that implementable on a consistent basis? Implementation, beyond mere rhetoric, requires sophisticated prioritization analysis, application of cost–benefit analysis models, and recognition of the degree and nature of the threat.

It is, after all, impossible for government (regardless which level) to act—proactively or reactively—to *all* threats. This is why prioritization regarding resource allocation is of such overwhelming importance. However, more important is the articulation and implementation of a national cybersecurity policy. However, here too the policy is insufficient; the test is how realistic is its implementation. This requires hard choices by government, law enforcement, corporate leaders, and the public.

This takes me back to the conversation with the vice president for corporate security: his delineation between large corporations and midsize–small corporations is, perhaps, reflective of an uncomfortable reality. This reality cuts across distinct audiences, all relevant to this discussion. However, there is, in addition to the reality of "just how much government can do," a flip side best articulated as broad based, institutionalized cooperation in response to the threat posed by cybersecurity.

The theme of cooperation has been a center piece throughout this book. This is not by chance. As mentioned in Chapter 1, I served as legal advisor to a congressional task force regarding U.S. Homeland Security policy. The principle of cooperation was uppermost in my mind, particularly the profound lack of cooperation, both inter and intra: inter between agencies and distinct constituencies, intra among a particular agency.

Both forms of cooperation are essential to developing—and implementing—effective cyber countersecurity. The examples and vignettes interspersed throughout this book are intended to facilitate the reader's understanding of the need to develop institutionalized cooperation and, simultaneous to that, recognizing the difficulty in such an effort.

The reasons are varied; the rationalizations are offered. Whether it is financially driven as is the case with corporations or *turf* and budget as was explained to me by law enforcement officials, the consequences are clearly predictable. The beneficiary of a consistent lack of cooperation is the wrong doer; the victims are plentiful.

It is worthwhile recalling my conversation with a corporate executive referenced in Chapter 1. In essence, the corporation assumed a risk when it deliberately underinvested in cyber protection. This decision, seemingly, reflected client apathy regarding the possible consequences of a cyber attack. The financial ramifications to the corporation—according to the executive tasked with handling the fallout—are, in his words, *very significant.* The negative repercussions to clients are, similarly, significant.

That seemingly calculated decision is problematic. It reflects a failure to directly confront the threat. It also leaves unresolved the question regarding the extent of government involvement either proactively or retroactively.

This is in a direct contrast to a meeting that I held in Israel with a leading cyber expert. The conversation was extraordinarily insightful, shedding light on the intersection between national security and cybersecurity. More importantly, it highlighted the crucial role government can—and should—play with respect to cyber.

Our conversation focused on questions of law and policy; the technical matters, while undoubtedly important, were not at the forefront of what we discussed. What particularly impressed me—in the context of cooperation—was the enormous benefit accrued, when public and private sectors joined forces and cooperated.

That is not intended as a gloss over inevitable tensions, jealousies, and competition between the two. It was, however, in sharp contrast to the discussions I had with U.S. law enforcement officials. The difference between the two approaches was jarring. The consequences are obvious. It is for that reason that the theme of cooperation occupies such importance in this book.

In Chapter 1, I used the term *new frontier.* I mitigated the *positive* generally associated with the term by noting the commensurate with benefits are the, inevitable, nefarious uses of cyber. Needless to say, those are dangerous and harmful and oftentimes are realized too late. There is, as we have come to learn, much harm that directly emanates from cyber. Examples abound on a daily basis. Many of us have been victims of harm, whether on a personal, professional, or community basis. Our vulnerability to cybercrime is well documented; there is no need to repeat the litany of incidents, ranging from the irritating to the truly catastrophic.

It is clear that individuals in groups, worldwide, are dedicated to continuously seek ways in which to use cyber to their advantage and to our disadvantage. There is, truly, a *us–them* with respect to cyber. The harms posed by cybercriminals and cyberterrorists are significant; of greater concern are future harms they are, undoubtedly, planning to impose on society. Of that, I have no doubt.

In addition to the overwhelming importance of, and benefit accrued from, cooperation for this book has addressed a number of other relevant issues. We have also explored critical questions regarding protection; that is, how should corporations protect themselves and what is the role of the nation-state in response to attacks on corporate entities. In doing so, we have focused on important legal and policy considerations with a particular focus on the application—and limits—of self-defense.

As noted above, there is a profound lack of consensus regarding the question of government involvement. Perhaps as a direct reflection of my background in the Israel Defense Forces, I am frankly baffled by the hesitation repeatedly expressed to me regarding the role of government in cyber protection. I believe that cyber attacks need to be perceived as similar to physical attacks.

The consequence of that, for me, is clear: An attack on an American corporation warrants government response. Although that requires the cooperation discussed above, the benefits—short and long term alike—significantly outweigh any negative consequences regarding government *over* involvement. Frankly, the stakes are too high to resort to tired clichés and irrelevant mantras regarding privacy concerns, that is, not to minimize the question of privacy—NSA leaks disturbingly highlight the reality of government intrusion—but it is to suggest that cyber threats require a balanced and nuanced approach. Summarily dismissing government involvement is short sighted and ultimately counterproductive.

That principle was abundantly clear to me while serving in the Israel Defense Forces and has been powerfully reinforced while researching and writing this book. Hand-in-hand with government involvement is the question of self-defense. In actuality, the two are directly related and cannot be separated from one other.

Self-defense is a critical question in the cyber discussion. The inquiry is whether the nation-state owes a duty to corporations and individuals, who have been victimized by a cyber attack. It is not an abstract question but one rather intended as a concrete query. The answers, as my conversations with a wide range of individuals highlighted, are unclear.

While an easy answer is *yes*, it is far more complicated than that. Similarly *no* is an unacceptable response, because national interests do justify state involvement in cybersecurity even when state targets are not directly attacked.

Therefore, the answer lies somewhere in the middle.

In my classes, whether *Global Perspectives on counterterrorism* or *Criminal Procedure*, I emphasize to students that the most important word in discussing the tensions between legitimate individual freedom rights and equally legitimate national security public order rights is balance. I refer to it as the *B* word.

Balance is hard to define and undoubtedly difficult to apply. In the context of state obligation to corporations and individuals, it would be an impractical *stretch* to impose on government the obligation to respond to every cyber attack. This suggestion is a nonstarter from the beginning. Conversely, to suggest government owes no duty violates the social contract that is the underpinning of civil society. This, too, is a *nonstarter*.

There are great risks in imposing *response* burdens on the nation-state in the aftermath of a cyber attack. If the attack can be traced back to state agents of another country, then legitimate questions arise regarding the limits of sovereignty, self-defense, and conflict. These are extraordinarily important questions with powerful consequences, regardless of how the reader suggests their resolution.

It is incumbent upon us to push forward the discussion regardless of how difficult and uncomfortable it is. Bruised egos are to be damned: the threat posed is simply too great.

Glossary of terms

Computer network An information structure used to permit computers to exchange data. The infrastructure may be wired, wireless (e.g., Wi-Fi), or a combination of the two.

Critical infrastructure Physical or virtual systems and assets under the jurisdiction of a state that are so vital that their incapacitation or destruction may debilitate a state's security, economy, public health, or safety, or the environment.

Cyber attack A deliberate and direct aggressive action intended to harm critical infrastructure. Further, a cyber attack is any deliberate attempt to compromise the confidentiality, integrity, or availability of data, resources, or processes through the use of electronic means.

Cyber counterattack Use of a cyber weapon intended to harm a designated target in response to an attack.

Cyber professionals Those engaged in never-ending efforts to counterminimize cyber threats to their customers and clients.

Cyber threat The possibility of action or an incident in the cyber domain which, when materialized, jeopardizes some operation dependent on the cyber world.

Cyber warfare Usage of cyber capacity of a sufficient scale, during a determined period in high speed, to reach certain objectives in or through cyberspace, these actions being considered as a menace for the targeted state.

Cybercrime Criminal activity conducted using computers and the Internet, often financially motivated. Cybercrime includes identity theft, fraud, and Internet scams, among other activities. Cybercrime is distinguished from other forms of malicious cyber activity, which have political, military, or espionage motivations.

Cybercriminal An individual who commits cybercrimes, where he/she makes use of the computer either as a tool or as a target or as both.

Cybersecurity   The effort to protect information, communications, and technology from harm caused either accidentally or intentionally; important to emphasize that a cyber attack is profoundly distinct from a physical attack. Further, cybersecurity is the effort to ensure the confidentiality, integrity, and availability of data, resources, and processes through the use of administrative, physical, and technical controls.

Cyberterrorism   The politically motivated use of computers and information technology to cause severe disruption or widespread fear in society.

Cyberterrorist   One who engages in cyberterrorism.

Firewalls   Parts of a computer system or network that are designed to block unauthorized access while permitting outward communication.

Foreseeable threats are those that will be carried out in near future (with no specificity); therefore, they are more distant than an imminent threat. For example, a foreseeable threat would be premised on valid intelligence indicating terrorists will shortly begin bringing explosives onto airplanes in liquid substances.

Geopolitics   To relate between nation-states and their engagement with the larger global community with particular emphasis on the relationship between geography and nation-state politics.

Hacking   Using a computer to gain unauthorized access to data in a system.

Imminent threats are those that are to be shortly conducted; as an example, a hostile intelligence report suggests that a bomb will be detonated tomorrow at 9:11 a.m. at a domestic terminal at JFK airport.

Long-range threats are threats that may reach fruition at an unknown time; for example, terrorists' training with no operational measure specifically planned would fit in this category.

Patriot Act   An act passed by Congress after the September 11, 2001 attacks designed to provide law enforcement agencies with the ability and tools needed to prevent future terrorist attacks. The USA Patriot Act took into account laws that were already on record and made adjustments to preserve the liberty and lives of American citizens both stateside and abroad. Also called: Uniting and Strengthening America by Providing Appropriate Tools Required to Intercept and Obstruct Terrorism.

Section 51 of the United Nations Charter   An article of the United Nation's Charter that recognizes *the inherent right of individual or collective self-defense* by anyone.

Stuxnet is a malicious computer worm believed to be a jointly built American–Israeli cyber weapon.

Suicide bombing A terrorist bombing carried out by someone who does not hope to survive it.

Terrorism An act, by an individual or a group, intended to kill innocent individuals, primarily as a way of instilling fear in others, with the purpose of advancing one of the four causes—political, religious, social, and cultural—with respect to government policy.

The five actors in traditional terrorism

> **The bomber** The person recruited to do the bombing.
>
> **The cell leader** Engages and attracts other members to join their cause.
>
> **The financier** Acquires the money to fund the operation.
>
> **The person responsible for logistics** Controls operations, including the purchase of cell phones, weapons, investigative resources, cars, and so on.
>
> **The person who creates the environment contributing to the legitimacy of suicide bombing** Creates such an environment to make the greatest statement.

Uncertain threats constitute those that invoke general fears of insecurity. As a result of train bombings in England and Spain, travelers in the United States might potentially or conceivably feel insecure riding trains without bolstered security. This would be true regardless of whether there is valid intelligence indicating terrorists intend to target trains in the United States.

Vignettes Short written descriptions.

References and suggestions
for further reading

Am. Civil Liberties Union v. Clapper, 785 F.3d 787 (2d Cir., 2015).

Barrett, D. *Surveillance Court Judge Criticized NSA 'Overcollection' of Data*, The Wall Street Journal (August 11, 2014), http://www.wsj.com/articles/surveillance-court-judge-criticized-nsa-overcollection-of-data-1407806807.

Betters, E. *Sony Pictures Hack: Here's Everything We Know About the Massive Attack So Far*, Pocket Lint (February 5, 2015, 5:55 PM), http://www.pocket-lint.com/news/131937-sony-pictures-hack-here-s-everything-we-know-about-the-massive-attack-so-far.

Carr, J. *Inside Cyber Warfare: Mapping the Cyber Underworld* (2nd ed., 2011).

Chapter VII: Action with respect to threats to the peace, breaches of the peace, and acts of aggression, Charter of the United Nations, http://www.un.org/en/documents/charter/chapter7.shtml (last accessed on June 7, 2015).

Guiora, A. N. *The Resilient Homeland: How DHS Intelligence Should Empower America to Prepare for, Prevent, and Withstand Terrorist Attacks*, testimony at U.S. House of Representatives, Committee on Homeland Security (May 15, 2008).

Clarke, R. A. *Cyber War: The Next Threat to National Security and What to Do About It* (2012).

Die Hard 2. Dir. Renny Harlin. Perf. Bruce Willis. Twentieth Century Fox Film Corporation, 1990. Film.

Editorial Board et al. *A Blackout in Ukraine is a Reminder of the Dangers of Cyberattacks*, The Washington Post (November 18, 2016), https://www.washingtonpost.com/opinions/a-cautionary-blackout-in-ukraine/2016/02/17/da2d58ac-b4c5-11e5-9388-466021d971de_story.html?wpmm=1&wpisrc=nl_opinions.

Goodman, M. *Future Crimes: Inside the Digital Underground and the Battle for Our Connected World* (Reprint ed., 2016).

Guiora, A. N. Accountability and Effectiveness in Homeland Security, Social Science Research Network, http://papers.ssrn.com/sol3/papers.cfm?abstract_id=1090328.

Kaplan, F. *Dark Territory: The Secret History Of Cyber War* (2016).

Kuus, M. *Geopolitics Reframed: Security and Identity in Europe's Eastern Enlargement*, Palgrave MacMillan, 2007 as cited in Amos N. Guiora, Geopolitics.

Lewis, J. A. In Defense of Stuxnet, INSS (April 13, 2013), http://i-hls.com/2013/04/in-defense-of-stuxnet/.

Mazanec, B. M. *The Evolution of Cyber War: International Norms for Emerging-Technology Weapons* (2015).

O'Brien, R. D. and S. Shen. *The U.S., China, and Cybersecurity: The Ethical Underpinnings of a Controversial Geopolitical Issue*, Carnegie Council (May 24, 2014), http://www.carnegiecouncil.org/publications/articles_papers_reports/0156.

Rainie, L., Anderson, J., and J. Connolly. *Cyber Attacks Likely to Increase*, Pew Research Center (October 29, 2014), http://www.pewinternet.org/2014/10/29/cyber-attacks-likely-to-increase/.

Singer, P. W. and A. Friedman. *Cybersecurity and Cyberwar: What Everyone Needs to Know®* (1st ed., 2014).

Spivak, W. *Cyber Security Principles: Computer Security—Hazards and Threats* (2nd ed., 2015).

Stahl, L. *The Great Brain Robbery*, 60 Minutes (January 17, 2016), http://www.cbsnews.com/news/60-minutes-great-brain-robbery-china-cyber-espionage/.

Stempel, J. *NSA's Phone Spying Program Ruled Illegal By Appeals Court*, Reuters (May 7, 2015), http://www.reuters.com/article/2015/05/07/us-usa-security-nsa-idUSKBN0NS1IN20150507.

Valeriano, B. and R. C. Maness. *Cyber War: The Next Threat to National Security and What to Do About It* (1st ed., 2015).

Zetter, K. *An Unprecedented Look at Stuxnet, the World's First Digital Weapon*, Wired (November 3, 2014, 6:30 AM), http://www.wired.com/2014/11/countdown-to-zero-day-stuxnet/.

Zitun, Y. *IDF Establishes New Cyber Branch*, YNet News (June 15, 2015, 11:54 PM), http://www.ynetnews.com/articles/0,7340,L-4668912,00.html.

Index

Note: Page numbers followed by 'f' refer to figures.

Printed in the United States
by Baker & Taylor Publisher Services